About the Author

Calvin B. Hoover, who prepared this fifth report in the research series, has been Dean of the Graduate School of Arts and Sciences at Duke University since 1938. In 1947 he was Director of Research, Com. of the South. During the war years he was Chief of Economic Intelligence and Economic Advisor, U.S. Group, Control Council for Germany, 1945, and three years prior to that was in the Research and Analysis Division of O.S.S. He was formerly a Social Science Research fellow for study of the U.S.S.R.; Economic Advisor, Department of Agriculture; President, Southern Economic Association; Vice-President, Amer. Economic Association. He is author of GERMANY ENTERS THE THIRD REICH, ECONOMIC LIFE OF SOVIET RUSSIA, and DICTATORS AND DEMOCRACIES.

COMMITTEE FOR ECONOMIC DEVELOPMENT
RESEARCH STUDY

INTERNATIONAL TRADE AND DOMESTIC EMPLOYMENT

COMMITTEE FOR ECONOMIC DEVELOPMENT
RESEARCH STUDY

International Trade and Domestic Employment

BY

CALVIN B. HOOVER

Dean of the Graduate School of Arts and Sciences,
Duke University

First Edition
FOURTH IMPRESSION

New York   *London*

McGRAW-HILL BOOK COMPANY, INC.
1 9 4 5

THE MAPLE PRESS COMPANY, YORK, PA.

FOREWORD

THE deep interest of the Research Committee of the Committee for Economic Development in international economic relations is evidenced by the research studies that they have authorized and the policy statements that they have formulated in this field. In addition to this research staff monograph by Calvin B. Hoover, a study of cartels and international commodity agreements is being made by Edward S. Mason, and a supplementary paper on Russian-American relations has been prepared by Harold D. Lasswell. On their own account, the Research Committee have issued a special policy statement, *The Bretton Woods Proposals*, and a broader policy statement, *International Trade, Foreign Investment and Domestic Employment*.

These publications are part of a larger program of research and policy formulation focused on achieving and maintaining high levels of production and employment. A list of projects, completed and in process, is to be found on page 152.

This volume, *International Trade and Domestic Employment*, is intended for the layman. It sets forth in nontechnical language the basic principles involved in international production specialization and exchange, the important problems that we face currently in our foreign economic relations, and the lines of policy in dealing with these problems which promise best for our long-run welfare and for that of the world. At the same time, professional economists will find this book of interest because it shows how policy problems have spilled over into areas not encompassed in classical analysis.

THEODORE O. YNTEMA
Research Director

PREFACE

Until recently economic theory in international trade remained preeminently the field in which economists were in substantial agreement. The development of state-controlled and "mixed" economies alongside economies which, like our own, are still primarily laissez-faire economies has, however, introduced new complexities into this field. Consequently, it would not be fair to claim that the principles and policies outlined in this report reflect, even in a general way, the consensus of economists.

A substantial number of American economists would probably favor a simpler approach to the problems dealt with in this report. Their approach would be founded in principle upon the doctrine of free trade. Upon the basis of this doctrine they would presumably recommend that the United States simply remove all trade barriers and controls to the fullest extent possible.

It is even more worthy of note that most of the industrialists of the Committee for Economic Development with whom the author has discussed the subject would also favor the policy of removing protective tariffs and other barriers to trade as well as all state controls of international trade whenever this was at all possible. This represents a change in the attitude of American industrialists that might well deserve the appellation "historic." This change reflects, on the one hand, the confidence of American industrialists in their ability to produce and sell goods on the domestic and international market without the aid or protection of government. It represents also, the author believes, an effort on the part of American industrialists to align their position on foreign trade with their advocacy of free enterprise in domestic production and commerce.

Preface

In view of the position of many American industrialists and economists, I must personally accept the serious responsibility for advocating a policy and program that is, unfortunately, considerably more complex than would be appropriate for a world economy in which trade was still almost wholly between individuals living and producing in capitalistic countries characterized by free enterprise and nearly perfect competition.

My obligations to scores of economists, industrialists, government officials, and others who have read this manuscript or given me other substantial aid at the cost of much time and trouble to themselves are deep. Limitations of space prevent individual acknowledgment. In the course of this study I was fortunate enough to be able to spend some weeks in both London and Stockholm. The opportunity to consult with British and Swedish industrialists and economists and to view our foreign trade from a different angle was very useful.

Thanks are particularly due Professor Jacob Viner, who has read this study in several of its versions. His critical suggestions have been exceedingly useful. Professor James J. O'Leary gave me valuable assistance at one stage of the process of preparing some of the chapters for publication. I am also grateful to Dr. Gardiner Means, whose analytical understanding of complex theoretical problems encouraged me to persevere in trying to make heretical ideas understandable to someone besides myself. The assistance of Miss Sylvia Stone in the final stages of preparation of the manuscript has been of greatest value. Finally, if it had not been for the energy, sympathy, and persistence of Professor Theodore Yntema, it is exceedingly doubtful if this study would ever have been completed. For the final result, I take full responsibility.

CALVIN B. HOOVER.

DURHAM, N. C.,
May, 1945.

CONTENTS

Contents

SUMMARY OF MAJOR
RECOMMENDATIONS
AND CONCLUSIONS

THE CASE FOR OUR PARTICIPATION IN AN INTERNATIONAL PROGRAM TO EXPAND WORLD TRADE

As THE war draws to a close, the nations of the world are faced with the necessity of developing a policy and program for the revival and expansion of international trade. There can be little question but that the type of almost wholly unregulated international trade which flourished up to 1914, and which had been revived in some degree by 1929, would be ideal for the exchange of goods and services between capitalistic countries characterized by the free-enterprise system. In other words, if the present economic organization of most important countries were as nearly characterized by free enterprise as that of the United States, we might pattern the reorganization of postwar international trade on the pre-1914 system.

Up to the outbreak of the present war, however, the trend was decidedly away from *laissez faire* in international trade. This trend resulted from fundamental changes that had taken place in the economic systems of some of the most important countries, and it was accelerated enormously by the depression of the 1930's.

By 1933 Russia, Germany, and Japan had developed economies that were no longer characterized by *laissez faire* but were, on the contrary, wholly dominated by the state. State control of foreign trade for these countries was the inevitable corollary to state control of the domestic economy. In self-defense, other countries were often compelled to institute state control of their foreign trade.

· 1 ·

The state-controlled economies of Germany, Japan, and Italy are being destroyed by the war. We do not know what type of economic system will supersede these systems. Perhaps the trend toward state-controlled economies will now be reversed. Still, we must admit that in the various liberated countries political parties favoring extensive state control of the economy play a very prominent role. In France, for example, the state has taken over the coal mines and even General de Gaulle, who has been opposing the plans of the leftist parties for the nationalization of large-scale industry, has, in at least one formal statement, favored a planned economy. Even in Great Britain the concentrated control of industry and the strengthened role of the state are pronounced. In the words of Lord Halifax, British Ambassador to the United States, one of the major problems facing the postwar world is that of integrating the system of state trading in Russia, the system of free enterprise in the United States, and the system of free enterprise with certain modifications, which Britain hopes to maintain.[1]

The argument has been advanced that, in view of this development, there is no alternative to the acceptance of the prewar trend toward national controls of foreign trade. Indeed, it has been argued that the trend is inevitable and that foreign trade carried on directly by governments or by their agencies could most effectively expand the volume of international trade.

Objections advanced in the United States against the inevitability of the trend toward governmental foreign trade are, however, very strong. Fundamentally, the reasons for resisting the assumption that future foreign trade must be a function of national governments do not differ from the reasons that favor free capitalistic enterprise and oppose state ownership and operation of domestic industry and commerce. This is true in spite of the fact that state control of foreign trade does not impinge so directly upon the conduct

[1] Dispatch from the United Press, January 25, 1945, reporting a speech by Lord Halifax at Tallahassee, Fla.

of private and corporate enterprise as does state control of the domestic economy.

Examination of the record of nations with state controls of foreign trade does not support the conclusion that this is the system to which to harness our hopes for the revival and expansion of international trade. These national foreign-trade controls were operated from the viewpoint of the most immediate national self-interest. They took little account of the damage often inflicted upon the domestic economies of other nations. In their efforts to combat the catastrophic unemployment of the great depression or to protect a desperately weakened balance-of-payments position, many nations were compelled to supplement governmental controls of their domestic economies by similar control of their foreign trade. Often, these controls resulted in a form of competition for international markets aptly labeled the "beggar thy neighbor policy."

Normal channels of commerce were often blocked, making multilateral trade difficult if not impossible. Trade based upon natural comparative advantages of the different nations in producing goods and services was displaced. Under such circumstances, the greatest advantages of international specialization and division of labor could not be attained. A huge state bureaucracy was required to administer the trade controls, and an enormous proportion of the time and energy of the executives of industry and business was absorbed in dealing with red tape.

National control of foreign trade was often an instrument of domination of the economically weak by the strong. In the competition and bargaining between nations, which replaced international trade between individuals and corporations, a great temptation to place the weight of the sword in the balance was often not resisted.

However unfortunate the ultimate effects upon international trade, these import-export controls did, when combined with domestic controls of the national economies, relieve domestic unemployment considerably. Although under these controls the volume of international trade during the late 1930's approached the predepression levels, in most countries of the world it did not revive in proportion to the growth of national incomes during the same period.

Because of these experiences, most nations appear stubbornly resolved not to expose their postwar domestic markets to foreign aggression by unilateral devaluation of currencies, exchange control, export subsidies, and the like. Indeed, this feeling has progressed so far that few countries show any willingness to expose their domestic economies in the postwar world even to the effects of wholly unregulated international trade.[1]

In consequence, the alternative to rigid and potentially predatory national foreign-trade controls is not likely to be found in an effort, almost certainly abortive, to induce countries to remove such controls completely as a free act of international good will. However, international bargains resulting in cooperative agreements for the removal of some controls and for the elimination of the more objectionable features of those remaining appear capable of attainment. Nations retaining some controls can be expected to recognize the advantages of an agreement on internationally recognized working rules with respect to the operation of these controls.

Above all, international institutions for facilitating and regulating world trade will need to be provided to supplement or supplant national controls. It is possible that in most countries a postwar period of full employment will eventually make possible the relaxation or removal of national foreign-trade control on a scale much beyond immediate prospects.

The nature of the system of international trade after the war will, of course, not be determined by purely economic

[1] Thus Lord Keynes, for example, found it necessary to give categoric assurance to the British Parliament that he has not tied the pound so securely to the dollar that British capacity to maintain full employment might be impaired.

forces. If the coming peace seems only a truce, while the nations rearm and choose sides for a new conflict, national controls of foreign trade will certainly be continued. If, on the contrary, the peace offers a good prospect of permanency, there will be an extraordinary opportunity for international cooperation to restore a larger measure of freedom in international trade.

We cannot possibly know now whether the coming peace settlement will present this opportunity. *But there are strong reasons for developing our national policy in the field of international trade on the assumption that the form of world organization arising out of the peace settlement will provide the necessary international security for a freer flow of international trade.* Should this hope fail, our position in international trade would not be immediately critical; we would have adequate time to adjust our policy to meet the control policies of other nations, were that necessary. If, however, we do not give evidence of our support of a policy of international cooperation in facilitating world trade, the opportunity for such cooperation may never materialize.

Both national self-interest and humanitarian considerations demand the participation of the United States in an international program that would facilitate a greater volume of interchange of goods and services to mutual economic advantage. It is true that such a program will not be achieved without overcoming great difficulties and without making sacrifices that partially subtract from its advantages. But if the essential elements of the program could be put into operation, we would increase our total national income through the benefits of international specialization and division of labor. *The United States should offer leadership in such a program.* In the Atlantic Charter, in the lend-lease agreements, in the speeches of President Roosevelt, Vice President Wallace, and Secretary Hull, we have repeatedly given other countries reason to expect much from us on this score. Conservative elements in the United States that have differed sharply with the administration on domestic issues have supported strongly such an international program.

The great superiority in our standard of living over that of most other countries causes those countries to look to the United States for leadership in international measures to better living standards. Among other things, reiteration by American officials and publicists of the principle that raw materials should be accessible to all countries on an equal footing has aroused great expectations.

Without the United States it is most unlikely that substantial progress could be made by other countries in an international program for the mitigation of trade barriers and the development of international institutions to further world trade. Should we not enter into such a program, or should such a program fail to eventuate for any reason, a system of trading blocs, based upon economic and geographical considerations as in the former sterling area, would probably be formed. Political friction resulting from competition for raw materials and markets under such conditions might easily be accompanied by the growth of political as well as economic rivalry with the United States.

Our participation in a program for facilitating world trade would be a major step toward maintenance of peace in the postwar world. The prospects for a sustained advance in the living standards of most countries would be greatly improved. Higher standards of living for substantially all countries would provide a most favorable climate for other forms of peaceful international collaboration. The existence of institutions furthering full international trade should reduce the forces pushing toward nationalistic control of domestic economies. Failure to carry out such a program might well have the opposite effect.

A SEVEN-POINT PROGRAM

The essential elements of American participation in a program for the expansion of international trade and for freeing this trade from the more constricting and objectionable forms of national control would be:

1. Participation in a plan for stabilization of currencies.

2. Participation in an international bank to provide loans for reconstruction and development.

3. Securing international agreements for the elimination, insofar as possible, of international cartels, which are among the most objectionable barriers to trade. To the extent that elimination proves unfeasible, effective national and international regulation of cartels should be provided.

4. Lowering our protective tariff in a substantial degree in return for reciprocal action by other countries, and refraining from using the tariff as a means of fending off foreign competition for our war-born industries.

5. Settlement of lend-lease on a basis that would not disrupt the general structure of the international balance of payments.

6. Determination of our mercantile marine policy on the basis of minimum requirements of national security, of comparative cost of service, and of concern for equilibrium in the international balance of payments.

7. *Carrying out dynamic measures for attaining and maintaining a high level of domestic employment, while collaborating in international economic policies that would facilitate the attainment and maintenance of high levels of employment by other countries. This is the most essential element in the program.*

Reciprocal concessions and obligations by other countries would, of course, be a condition of our undertaking the first six steps of this seven-point program.

1. *The United States should participate in the international monetary fund blueprinted at the Bretton Woods conference.* This fund provides for international currency stabilization. Free fluctuation of foreign-exchange rates might appear to be a solution for the dilemma created by the coexistence of controlled national economies and free international trade. In practice, the national interests of individual countries rarely permit free fluctuation of the international value of their

currencies. Consequently, the choice lies between national exchange controls and some form of an international stabilization agreement. Without some means for agreement between nations on exchange rates, reciprocal agreements to reduce tariffs and other trade barriers become impracticable, since currency depreciation is at least temporarily an effective substitute for tariff barriers. The International Monetary Fund constitutes an effort to achieve currency stabilization without strait-jacketing exchange rates.

The ratio between the pound and the dollar set by a stabilization agreement should be such as to permit a larger net flow of goods and services to the United States. Such a ratio might help to correct our prewar tendency toward a net export surplus and the British prewar tendency toward a net import surplus.

2. *To restore production and trade in the world, the United States should take the necessary steps toward participation in the International Bank for Reconstruction and Development.* The United States should not strive for so large a net export of goods and services that it would subsequently require repayments, *i.e.,* imports of goods and services, greater than we would be willing to accept or the debtor countries would want to furnish. The pronounced tendency of our economy to overexport and underimport must be counteracted, not merely by lowering our trade barriers or by relative appreciation of the dollar in the foreign-exchange market, *but to a much greater extent by increasing purchasing power on our domestic market.* Stability and an equilibrium with respect to both our international trade and investment should be top requisites of action either on our own national initiative or through international agreement.

Should we have an export surplus of goods and services, we must be prepared to make approximately equivalent investments abroad or the export surplus will cease, quite likely with the accompaniment of an international economic crisis. If we do not invest sufficiently to match the surplus in our balance of payments, other countries will have deficits in their means of payment for import surpluses and will be forced to restore exchange control and other trade barriers or to devalue their currencies. Such depreciation of national currencies would present the gravest problem to any international plan for currency stabilization.

It seems unlikely that the flow of private capital from the United States or from other countries immediately after the war will be sufficient either to meet the needs of countries seeking loans or to finance a continuing net export balance of American goods during the reconstruction period abroad. Means might be found for stimulating the lending of capital funds, but a serious financial crisis would loom ahead unless there were also provisions to limit loans to the borrowing country's ability to meet its obligations in foreign exchange when payments of interest and principal came due. An international institution for encouraging and guiding the flow of international investment, such as that agreed upon at Bretton Woods in the plan for the International Bank for Reconstruction and Development, would go far toward meeting this situation.

3. *No program for the removal of barriers and controls in international trade should be carried out in disregard of the cartel problem.* Cartelization of industry, which in many countries received an immense impetus from the depression, has been accelerated and strengthened by the war. Many of the undesirable purposes served by tariffs, exchange control, and other forms of trade barriers have also been achieved by means of cartels. Ideally, international action for effectively freeing the channels of international trade should outlaw cartels in international trade, but this drastic solution is unlikely to be feasible. Provisions should be made for regulating cartels to the extent necessary to prevent emasculation of any program for freer international trade. Registration should be required for all agreements between American corporations and foreign corporations or governments that might involve restraint of trade. An international conference is recommended to

negotiate an agreement on national and international policies with respect to cartels. A permanent international regulatory institution might develop from such an investigation.

4. *The United States should substantially lower its protective tariff, contingent on reciprocal action by other countries.* Our standard of living is raised by exchanging goods and services that we produce most efficiently for those produced more efficiently by other countries. If we can import more cheaply than we produce, we should do so unless there are compelling reasons to the contrary. A program of reduction of international trade barriers would increase competition in our domestic market and reduce tendencies toward monopoly in our price structure. The influx of foreign-produced goods into our wholesale and retail markets would require competing American producers to lower their prices and, where possible, their costs of production. Those who could not produce at costs low enough to compete with imported goods would have to transfer to the production of other goods, perhaps to goods required in larger volume to satisfy the increased export demand resulting from a lowered tariff.

This would not be wholly without risk or difficulties. Under conditions of depression or of threatened depression, the probable increased flexibility of prices might be an added source of instability in the domestic price structure. To the degree that the lowering of our protective tariff increases purchasing power for American goods in foreign markets, employment in industries producing for export would rise. However, this might not offset immediately the loss of employment in industries less sheltered by the tariff than in the past. Governmental assistance should be provided to industries and areas which can show that their position has been rendered difficult by tariff reduction. Such aid should be provided particularly in the case of temporarily displaced labor. It should also be forthcoming in the case of the family-sized farm where distress is caused by the lowering of the protective tariff on farm products.

Summary of Major Recommendations

The reciprocal trade-agreements program should be utilized to lower national tariffs and other trade barriers until a multilateral international agreement can be worked out. Since it will otherwise expire this year, the life of the Reciprocal Trade Agreement Act should be extended.

Reciprocal action by other countries in lowering trade barriers does not imply our exacting an equivalent reduction by other countries as a condition for agreement. Our balance-of-trade situation and our generally strong economic position make it feasible for us to reduce trade barriers more drastically than may be expedient for some countries. The United States should propose an international conference for the multilateral reduction of trade barriers. We should offer a substantial cut in our protective tariff as a part of this proposed international program for lowered trade barriers.

5. *Lend-lease, a law enacted in the interest of national defense in a world at war, should not be used to serve other purposes. Lend-lease should be regarded as a cost of war, and repayment for goods and services consumed during the war should not be required.* Lend-lease should not be continued after the close of hostilities. Financial assistance, if extended to any country after the war, should be upon the basis of new arrangements. Decisions with respect to such loans should be made by Congress after weighing economic and political considerations not to be confused with the immediate military considerations that motivated lend-lease. The more than $40 billion worth of material advanced by the United States government through lend-lease, insofar as it has been expended by the recipient governments, should be considered a war expense and repayment should not be demanded. A policy requesting repayment of a major portion of lend-lease would disrupt hopelessly the international balance of payments; it would poison with international ill will the whole postwar period.

Lend-lease materials of value for peacetime purposes, in existence abroad after victory or on order in this country, should be sold by the United States government to the highest bidder. The proceeds should, of course, accrue to the United States Treasury. The principle should be firmly established that all goods received after cessation of hostilities are to be paid for. Naturally, such goods should not be permitted to be re-exported to the United States. A considerable portion of these supplies could serve relief purposes, sold rather than given, wherever sale is possible. All ships chartered to other nations under lend-lease should be turned back to the United States, disposal of these ships to be determined by our general mercantile marine policy.

6. *Our merchant marine policy should be founded upon three major considerations: first, national security; second, comparative cost; third, stability of the international balance of payments.* If it could be operated profitably without subsidy, there should be no limitation upon the size of our merchant marine. From the purely economic standpoint, however, we could get along with an even smaller merchant marine than that which we possessed before the war, since we can hire our shipping more cheaply than we can furnish it. From the standpoint of national security, however, we must maintain a substantial mercantile marine as well as yards in which ships can be built.

It is extremely difficult to determine the minimum of merchant shipping necessary for national defense. A merchant marine of not more than 12 million deadweight tons of new fast ships available for active service, plus a laid-up reserve of 10 million tons, capable of quick reconditioning, might be expected to meet all reasonable needs of national security. To keep this efficient, newly built fleet fully employed would require expanding the tonnage carried by our own merchant marine substantially beyond that of the prewar period. (A considerable portion of our prewar merchant tonnage of some 12 million deadweight tons was obsolescent, apart from the ships not in use at all.) This would leave some 38 million deadweight tons (depending upon when the war ended and when cuts in our shipbuilding program began) to be sold to other countries whose merchant marines have been depleted by the war.

We shall have to provide subsidies to operate the shipping which we retain. Additional subsidies will be needed to keep a portion of our shipbuilding industry in operation. This is part of the price of national security. Subsidies are required to enable shipbuilders and ship operators to pay wages on the American level in an industry where under present conditions we do not have a comparative advantage. We should not, however, allow our bill for subsidies to be any larger than necessary. We would do better to have part of our shipping done by foreign merchant fleets, since the cost would be so much lower. Money thus earned by merchant fleets of foreign ownership would be available to their countries as a means of payment for imports from the United States. A diminution in the earnings of foreign merchant fleets caused by the competition of an expanded American merchant marine subsidized by the government would to a corresponding extent reduce the purchasing power of foreigners for other American goods and services.

7. *The maintenance of a high level of employment in the United States is the most fundamental condition for keeping in operation a program of international trade expansion.* Evidence indicates that the level of our industrial activity is the greatest factor in determining the volume of our imports, on which many countries depend for their purchasing power in international trade. This is due primarily to the fact that a large part of our imports are raw materials and other goods used in further production. When our industry is operating at a high level, great amounts of these raw materials and semifinished goods are imported. Under conditions of depression these goods are imported in much smaller quantities almost regardless of how low the raw-material prices may go. In other words, during prosperity our imports are large; in depression, they are small.

Thus, curiously enough, the main order of causation

between foreign trade and domestic employment in this country is contrary to that claimed both by the advocates of tariff protection and by uncritical enthusiasts for foreign-trade expansion. If our national government stands ready to take strong internal measures, whenever necessary in time of depression or threatened depression, to maintain domestic employment, imports need not be feared as a cause of unemployment. On the other hand, expanding our exports should not be counted upon normally as a sovereign means of increasing domestic employment. It is true that under conditions of actual or threatened economic depression, measures aimed at contracting our imports and expanding our exports often would increase domestic employment if they were not offset by retaliatory measures on the part of other nations. Usually, however, such means for expanding our own employment would cause unemployment in other countries and would provoke counteraction.

Internal measures that expand domestic employment, provided they are not accompanied by restrictions on imports, result almost invariably in an expansion of the volume of international trade. This relation between domestic employment and international trade is not peculiar to the United States. It characterizes in some degree the economy of all other important capitalistic industrial countries.

The importance of the United States as a market for raw materials and other products of foreign countries is so great that, if depression ruled in the United States, prosperity in most other countries would be impossible unless they resorted to extremely close control of their foreign trade. Consequently, the volume of world trade is at present peculiarly dependent upon domestic employment in the United States.

Economic depression was the major cause for the growth of barriers and controls in international trade during the years preceding the present war. When faced by the fact or even serious threat of economic depression, hardly any country can be expected to refrain from trade controls. The maintenance of domestic employment at high levels in one country greatly aids the maintenance of domestic employment in other countries if it is done without dumping on foreign markets and without resort to import barriers. *The successful operation of a program for the relaxation and amelioration of national controls of foreign trade thus depends largely upon preventing world-wide depressions.*

OUR POSTWAR FOREIGN TRADE PROSPECTS

There will be a strong export demand for American products during the first few years after the end of the war with Germany. World inventories will need to be replenished and devastated areas reconstructed, and some of our peacetime competitors will temporarily be out of the market. Although Great Britain and some other countries in the war will have serious difficulties with their balance of payments, the gold holdings and dollar resources of most countries probably will ensure fairly adequate means of payment during this initial period. However, after this abnormal demand is satisfied, the underlying problems in the balance of payments will come to the forefront.

The future of world trade past the initial postwar period depends upon the success of the national programs of full employment to be initiated in practically all industrially advanced countries and upon the success of the programs of capital construction contemplated in many of the less industrialized countries.

It is highly desirable that the operation of these full-employment programs be facilitated by international economic cooperation in the expansion of world trade along the lines sketched above. It is true that under the most unfavorable combination of circumstances such a program for a compromise between national controls of the domestic economy and a large measure of freedom of international trade may in the actual event prove unworkable. It is of the utmost importance, however, that an energetic effort be made to formulate such a program and to put it in operation. If this failed and if nations should have to return to bilateral agreements, exchange control, bulk purchases by governmental agencies, and so on, it is desirable that there should be as little international acrimony and recrimination as possible with respect to the responsibility of any particular nation for failure in the effort.

The United States is exceedingly fortunate in having an economic position so strong that it can afford to take leadership in the movement toward freer international trade and to continue to support that movement as long as there is any reasonable hope for its success. The present prospect of its success is strong. We would be able to carry out a program of domestic full employment under almost any form of organization of world trade that might eventuate. Consequently, our national program to reach optimum levels of employment need not wait in fear of developments on the international economic scene. We should vigorously lead and support international economic cooperation, but we should not wait for its results before advancing equally vigorous domestic policies directed at attaining and maintaining the highest practicable level of employment.

I. THE DETERMINATION OF NATIONAL POLICY IN INTERNATIONAL TRADE

As the end of the war approaches we are confronted by a long series of interrelated questions concerning our policy in international trade.

What should be done about lend-lease? Should it be continued in any form after the fighting has ceased? Should it be repaid, at least in part? If so, how and in what form? In the actual goods lent, if they still exist, or in other goods and services? In cash, and if so, what sources of cash are there for the countries aided by lend-lease?

What should we do with our huge merchant marine built to satisfy war demands? Should we try to operate this fleet regardless of our higher costs? If we operate it, what will offset the loss of shipping receipts in the British balance of payments? If the loss is not made up, how will the British be able to purchase American cotton? If we sell the ships to other countries, how should payment be made?

What should we do with our new synthetic-rubber industry? Does national security allow us to abandon it even if it proved impossible to produce synthetic rubber as cheaply as crude rubber could be imported? If part of the industry is to be kept in operation for security reasons, how will we reconcile its higher costs? By a high tariff? By import quotas? By a government subsidy?

What use should we make of our huge "surplus" industrial capacity in machine tools, airplanes, aluminum, and magnesium? What about our agricultural "surpluses"? Can foreign markets be found for them? We know that we could sell more abroad if it were not for trade barriers and controls.

· 17 ·

Will other countries lower their trade barriers if we are willing to reduce ours?

What tariff policy should our government pursue after the war? Do our tariffs actually keep out large quantities of foreign goods? Would we hazard unemployment if our tariff were lowered and more foreign goods came in? Should we undertake a program of substantial tariff cuts to induce other countries to remove their restraints on trade? Or should we continue with only a further development of our reciprocal trade-agreements program?

What should be done about the rebuilding of war-devastated countries? What about the development of the non-industrialized countries—the South American countries, Africa, the Near East, China? Should international loans be provided? Should they be made in gold, in credit, or in goods? Should they be wholly intergovernmental transactions or entirely or partially privately financed? Should the United States participate in the International Bank for Reconstruction and Development as proposed by representatives of the United Nations at Bretton Woods?

Should we also participate in the proposed International Monetary Fund? What domestic and international advantages are to be gained from such participation? Is there any prohibitive disadvantage?

What should be our postwar policy toward international cartels? Will we face cartelized competition from abroad? Could an international body regulate cartel activities in the interests of expanding world trade?

These problems can hardly be solved independently of each other. Somehow we must evolve a national policy that will enable us to reach solutions that are reasonably consistent or at least not in direct conflict with one another. We have acquired an unenviable reputation for disrupting international trade by trying to sell as much as possible while attempting to purchase a minimum. A postwar policy combining maximum tariff protection with an aggressive sales policy in foreign markets through subsidies, export credits, and high-pressure salesmanship would contribute materially to international ill will and economic confusion.

Public sentiment in the United States today strongly favors wholesale removal of restrictions on international trade. Many persons are convinced that trade barriers and controls were among the causes of the great depression of the 1930's. Many believe that piling up of international trade barriers has been an important cause of wars in general and the present war in particular, and that continuation of these barriers and controls will lead to another world war. To these reasons for the reorganization of international trade are added the simple human arguments that "all peoples should have access to raw materials" and that "we should not slaughter little pigs while the Chinese are starving."

We have come to recognize, chiefly as a lesson of the recent depression, that neither specific problems nor our general national policy in international trade and investment can be resolved independently of the even more basic and more pressing problem of maintaining domestic employment at the highest practicable level.[1] This must be emphasized, because only since the experiences of the 1930's have economists fully appreciated the close relationship between international trade and the level of domestic employment *under conditions of depression or threatened depression.* The strict controls erected during the 1930's by almost all nations except the United States to regulate their foreign trade reflected the growing recognition throughout the world of this functional relationship. These national controls were adopted in almost all the important industrial countries primarily as means for reducing domestic unemployment, even if this meant added

[1] This problem of the maintenance of domestic production and employment at optimum levels is the main reason for the existence of the Committee for Economic Development. Consequently, the solution of specific problems connected with our foreign trade and the development of a national policy and program in this field are of concern to the committee primarily in relation to the problem of optimum domestic employment.

unemployment in countries with which trade was carried on. The increased control of foreign trade was accompanied by and integrated with governmental control of most phases of domestic industry and commerce.

This trend toward governmental direction of economic life was neither originated nor maintained wholly on economic grounds. Even now, the question of its continuance or relaxation will not be determined exclusively by economic factors. Confidence in a peaceful postwar world must exist before any country will consent to the relaxation of national foreign-trade controls. If the threat of another war is dispelled while the first steps toward the resumption of international trade are taken, the way will be open for a positive program of international trade expansion. In turn, the possibility of a peaceful world will depend in considerable degree upon the success of such a trade program.

What are the relative advantages of a policy that would permit the removal or relaxation of national controls of foreign trade as compared with one that continued these controls? Is it feasible to remove these controls without providing alternative safeguards of national interests? In the answer to these questions should be found the solution for some of the specific problems listed at the beginning of this chapter as well as the guiding principles for a consistent national policy in our international trade.

THE ADVANTAGES OF INTERNATIONAL TRADE

1. Benefits from international trade are basically the same as those from domestic trade. If a program for expanding international trade were successfully implemented, the United States would gain through increased international specialization and division of labor. This would mean that we would expand production in lines in which our natural and capital resources, our skill in labor and management, and the development of our production techniques have given us an advantage over other countries. We would be exchanging the particular

goods we are able to produce at low cost for goods that other countries are equipped to produce at low cost.[1]

Since our natural and capital resources, our labor and management skills, and our engineering technique have resulted in high productivity of labor and high wages in the United States, under conditions of freer international trade we should exchange goods produced with relatively little labor for goods that required more labor. This would have the effect of expanding, for example, the potential market for our automobiles, while contracting perhaps the potential market for our textiles. If there were no counteracting effects, the net result would be an increase in our total national income. Expressed in different terms, this means that the cost of goods to consumers in the United States and also in the countries that traded with us would be lower.

Widening the market for a product through international trade makes possible the economies of large-scale production. This advantage is vitally important to small countries. The United Kingdom, for example, because of its relatively small domestic market, relies upon foreign trade not only to obtain raw materials and other commodities that cannot be produced at home but also to provide the wider markets which permit the utilization of mass-production methods. The United States is fortunate to possess many of the advantages accruing

[1] The increase in national income resulting from specialization and division of labor, made possible through international trade, has always been the keystone of legitimate arguments in favor of international trade. If the United States had reached a state in which it produced more than it could consume and had to export in order to get rid of surplus production, this argument would be invalid. It is true that at times, as in the depression of the 1930's, we have not been able to sell at going market prices all that we were able to produce. Under such circumstances, dumping goods abroad at less than domestic market prices, or even giving the goods away, might so stimulate business that the net result would be more advantageous to the country than if the goods were not produced at all. If, however, this inability to sell all we are able to produce were chronic and irreparable, as fortunately it is not, the whole theory of international trade would have to be revised. *Certainly if we were actually using international trade to offset our excessive capacity to produce national income, it would be nonsensical to offer ability of such trade to increase our national income as an advantage.*

from the interchange of commodities between areas. This country is a vast free-trade area, providing a huge domestic market, in contrast to Europe where national boundaries break up the continent into many small areas and decrease the relative amount of intracontinental trade.

As far as the United States is concerned, our often prohibitive protective tariff has reduced the imports of manufactured goods to very low levels. This has stimulated the development of our less efficient manufacturing industries. It has been a contributing factor in keeping foreign countries chronically poor in American dollar exchange, and has thus limited export markets both for our agricultural products and for manufactures that could compete in price or quality on the international market. The protective tariff has also denied American consumers the advantage of the lower prices that would result if some cheaper foreign-made goods were permitted entry.

2. Increased international trade brought about by reduction of tariff barriers would mean intensified competition for American industries producing goods that compete with imported commodities. This would lower prices to consumers and, in some cases, lower production costs through enforced increase in efficiency. Furthermore, the increased competition would provide a check on monopolies in American industry. Obviously, this would be an advantage to consumers, but a disadvantage to particular producers who must sell their goods in competition with goods imported from abroad. This disadvantage would be offset, however, by a parallel advantage to producers for the export market.

3. The wider market resulting from an expanded international trade would offer more foreign buyers for goods in the production of which we have excess facilities and a comparative advantage, such as aluminum and machine tools. We would not thereby be "solving our problem of general overproduction," for we should have to find a market for the goods eventually sent us in payment unless we, in effect, gave the

exported goods away. It does mean that certain of our industries with surplus capacity would find abroad a larger receptivity for their products if foreign countries were able to gain American dollars by selling their goods on our expanded domestic market. Thus, selling increased quantities of, say, aluminum in foreign markets will depend on our increased imports and on our granting credit abroad.

4. Through freer international exchange of goods and services we should be able to improve materially the standard of living in other countries and in our own. To countries dependent upon foreign trade for raw materials, for food, for capital equipment, or for consumption goods not readily produced domestically, gains through international trade can be considerable. We have given the countries of the world repeated assurances that we would help raise the world-wide standard of living. Successful concerted action for increasing the international exchange of goods and services would be a major step in this direction.

5. A world in which all countries could carry on unobstructed international trade under international regulation would be less likely to produce conflicts than a world in which each nation, through its governmental control of foreign trade, competes with every other nation for the most favorable bargain.[1] Prior to the growth of national controls of international trade, whatever regulation did exist was largely automatic. If some degree of automatic regulation could be restored, with international direction and regulation initiated where and when essential, some of the causes for conflict between nations would be eliminated.

6. The basic arguments for the maximum degree of *laissez faire* attainable are as profoundly significant in relation to

[1] In the interest of simplicity, the advantages and disadvantages of freer international trade have been compared with the advantages and disadvantages of national controls of foreign trade. In actual practice, as is pointed out later, the choice is not so simple. It lies between the more extreme forms of national control, on the one hand, and some degree of international control, combined with a minimum of national control, on the other.

international trade as in relation to the domestic economy. More important than the question of the relative efficiency of private and corporate enterprise, as compared with industry and commerce controlled by the state, is the still unsolved problem of whether human liberty can be preserved in a state-owned and -operated economy. It is difficult to measure how far we could move toward state control in any given direction before curtailment of personal liberty would become a problem. While, paradoxically enough, the very maintenance of freer enterprise may depend upon the extension of state control in a particular instance, the basic arguments against extension of state control must always weigh heavily in the scale.

FREEING INTERNATIONAL TRADE FROM NATIONAL CONTROLS

Since the advantages of a larger flow of international trade are so well known, why were interferences with freedom of international trade allowed to develop? Most restraints upon international trade that existed prior to 1914 were caused by the predominance of special interests over national welfare. The consumers' interest in lower prices offered little by way of political opposition to particular producers seeking tariff protection. American interference with freedom of international trade, primarily through the maintenance of tariff protection, has not been planned as part of a conscious national policy. Instead, our tariff has grown in piecemeal fashion, reflecting largely the political power and shrewdness of the representatives of each protected industry.[1]

If the whole case against freedom of international trade reflected simply the opposition of special interests to the general good, there could be no honest reason why we should not proceed forthwith to remove, unilaterally if necessary,

---

[1] This is not to deny that there may have been a national advantage in the acceleration of the industrialization of our economy, caused by our protective tariff.

all restraints upon international trade introduced by the United States. Indeed, many economists advocate this policy. However, the matter is not nearly so simple; on the contrary, serious difficulties and complexities exist.

1. Unfortunately one cannot lay down the simple rule that the national interest is invariably served if a country's citizens are permitted to buy where goods and services can be obtained most cheaply. Prices measured in terms of national currencies do not always reflect real comparative advantages in production. One country may be able to sell its goods in the market of another because other factors may have arbitrarily or temporarily reduced the money price. In the case of outright dumping, for example, a country may subsidize the sale of its goods in another country. A temporary failure of foreign-exchange values to reflect the true purchasing-power parities of currencies may produce a similar result. This might come about through deliberate devaluation of its currency by the exporting country, or it might result, in spite of governmental efforts to prevent it, from speculation in the country's currency.

A similar effect might occur if a foreign cartel sold its product in our domestic market at a price that forced American producers out of business and then raised the price. Indeed, where administered or monopolistic prices prevail, there is a noticeable tendency for corporations engaged in production requiring heavy fixed investment to sell their products abroad at lower net prices than they receive at home. They can afford this, provided the export price covers additional costs and does not interfere with the maintenance of the domestic market price. A protective tariff in the country of manufacture is helpful in this process, but it is not essential.

Finally, money prices may fail to reflect real differences in comparative production advantages because of differences in pricing and cost accounting. In the chemical industry, for example, a particular product may be treated as a major product in one country and as a by-product in another. The country which prices it as a by-product might place it on the international market at a lower quotation, but this would not reflect a real comparative advantage nor would the situation necessarily be permanent.

If selling below cost of production in any of its various forms were to continue permanently, in most instances it would mean only that the recipient country would obtain an addition to its consumable commodities at low real cost. If such selling were merely temporary, however, and if it resulted in disrupting the price structure and in shifting resources to other types of production in the importing country, the social and economic costs would outweigh any advantages of transitory cheapness.

2. If the country's domestic economy is in some degree a managed economy, state control of foreign trade may facilitate considerably the process of management. This is true even when the management of the domestic economy is only partial. To cite a mild example, even the maintenance of a desired general price level may be facilitated by state control of imports and exports, capital movements, and the like. The greater the degree of management of the domestic economy, the greater the consequent tendency to control foreign trade. The order of causation does not, however, operate nearly so strongly in the other direction. The long existence of a high protective tariff in the United States has not, for example, had any noticeable effect in producing direct state control of the domestic economy.

3. *Under conditions of economic depression, national controls of foreign trade can be used to alleviate domestic unemployment.* If widespread unemployment exists, a country usually can create additional employment opportunities by curtailing imports through tariffs, import quotas, exchange control, and associated measures, and by expanding exports through export subsidies, currency devaluation, and similar means. Such measures often result in a country's exporting its unemployment to other countries with which it trades. To the

extent that this is true, one country's gain is another's loss. Obviously, as long as this applies no one country can afford to reduce its national controls unless other countries agree to do likewise.

Moreover, it is often potentially dangerous for a country to refrain from national control of its foreign trade if there is serious danger of economic depression in countries that are its competitors in either its domestic or foreign markets. The country suffering from depression is likely to become the source of dumped exports. If the dumping is on a large enough scale, the country that has hitherto escoped depression may succumb also. The dwindling market for imported goods in the depressed countries may also accentuate the balance-of-payments difficulties of other countries. The adverse psychological effect of depression in any important country upon the financial markets of all others is also very important.

If prolonged and severe depressions are in the offing, the case for removal, or even relaxation, of national controls of foreign trade becomes greatly weakened. Conversely, any successful steps taken by countries through international cooperation to prevent economic depressions strengthen the case for greater freedom of international trade. It must be repeated that during the years immediately preceding the war a most important cause for the growth of national controls over foreign trade was the need for drastic measures against the catastrophic unemployment that accompanied the great depression. The proposed International Monetary Fund and International Bank for Reconstruction and Development constitute an attempt to establish institutions capable of dealing with the problems of economic depressions on an international level.

In the absence of such international institutions and without cooperation among nations, measures to combat economic depressions, naturally enough, have been national in character and scope. Although the measures taken by one nation were often injurious to another, scarcely any nation dared to refrain from protecting its interests by either offensive or defensive economic action. Domestic measures to combat deflation and to expand employment operated with more facility if foreign trade and finance were rigidly controlled. The case of Germany perhaps offers the most pertinent example. Germany's economic recovery from 1932 to 1939 took place under stringent control of both domestic industry and foreign trade. These measures made possible the carrying out simultaneously of large-scale expansion of industrial production, bank credit, and employment.

Without control of foreign trade to accompany the control of her domestic industry, Germany would have had great difficulty in putting through the economic expansion that she achieved prior to the present war, unless economic expansion of other important countries had been under way at the same time. In the absence of an international program of economic expansion and without national controls of her foreign trade, the measures taken by the German government to increase the purchasing power of her domestic market would have lost their effect through the draining off of newly created purchasing power by payments for increased imports and through capital flight.

Fear of inflation prevented use of the alternative device, *i.e.*, allowing the mark to depreciate. Indeed, it would have been difficult to maintain stability of prices, production costs, and wages, as well as the sustained demand for commodities essential to the German program of full production, if the Nazi government had been forced to rely solely upon the stimulative effects of a depreciated currency. This would have been so even if a non-Nazi government had been in power, inasmuch as the alternative of a cooperative, internationally sponsored program of full employment did not then exist.

During the depression, the United States was able to carry out a policy of expansion of purchasing power without resort to comprehensive controls of foreign trade. We did, of course, continue our protective tariff. We devalued the dollar and resorted to some other, minor measures. We did not have to rely on a system of comprehensive control of our foreign trade, primarily because of the relatively smaller importance of foreign trade to our whole economy and because the strength of our economic and financial position rendered us less vulnerable to depressive economic forces operating from outside. Likewise, we were not confronted by any difficulty in maintaining our balance of international payments. In other words, we did not have to worry about whether we would be able to pay for essential imports. This stronger economic and financial position permits the United States, under most probable circumstances, to obtain the advantages of international trade without protective controls. This relative invulnerability renders it feasible for us to take the initiative in international cooperation for the removal of the conditions that make national controls of foreign trade practically inevitable.

4. Serious problems are posed by the existence of controlled domestic economies, ranging from the completely nationalized, such as that of Soviet Russia, to the highly cartelized, as in Germany before the war or in Great Britain particularly since the war. The quasi-automatic processes that regulated international trade during a good part of the last century depended in large degree upon the operation of free competitive private enterprise both within the domestic economies of nations and in international trade. When the domestic economy of a country becomes nationalized or cartelized to a significant extent, it is inexact, to say the least, to speak of free international trade. Soviet Russia, for example, can accomplish by the mere decision of the state to buy or not to buy, to sell or to refrain from selling, all that other countries effect by protective tariffs, export subsidies, import quotas, exchange control, and all the other elaborate paraphernalia of national foreign trade control. It is by no means impossible for countries with relatively free domestic

economies to trade with those that have controlled, monopolistic, or nationalized industries, but the old system of unregulated international trade is hardly feasible any longer.

5. *Once protected industries have been established in a country, there is a social cost to be paid if the restoration of free trade drives the hitherto protected industry out of production.* For example, both sugar and wool production in the United States depend largely upon tariff protection. If this protection were withdrawn, the production of these commodities in the United States would probably be greatly curtailed. We could expect that total employment would not be affected, since the increased purchasing power of foreigners, resulting from increased sales of wool and sugar to us, would normally be used to purchase increased quantities of, say, machinery and perhaps raw cotton in the United States. The transfer of persons and capital from the production of wool and sugar to other employments would, however, involve a real social cost and would present serious adjustment problems for the areas producing these goods. In some cases it would be better for the national government to assume directly the social cost of facilitating the transfer of people and resources to other tyyes of production than to continue to subsidize high-cost production, through the expensive device of a high protective tariff, in industries lacking a natural comparative advantage.

6. *While unrestricted international trade facilitates the widest possible selection of goods and services for the individual, it does not distinguish between the essential and the nonessential in national welfare.* Thus, during the years immediately following the present war Great Britain probably will not permit individuals to purchase luxury goods abroad without limit, because almost all available foreign exchange will be needed to purchase raw materials, foodstuffs, and capital equipment.

Because of the depletion of their investments abroad, the accumulation of wartime indebtedness, and for other reasons, the British will experience great difficulty in paying for their imports. In these circumstances they must either export much more than before the war, or they must reduce their imports, or do both. If they are compelled to reduce their imports, they and other nations in a similar position are likely to follow the policy, "All must have bread before anyone has cake." Wheat, meat, timber, cotton, copper, and aluminum will have import preference over wines, fruits, silk stockings, automobiles, and radios.

China, India, some of the countries of Latin America, as well as others embarking upon programs of industrialization, are likely to inaugurate measures of control to ensure that out of the foreign exchange earned by the export of goods, the minimum amounts necessary to pay for their imports of essential capital equipment shall be made available. This may be done by import quotas, exchange control, protective tariffs, or by any of these in combination. To provide for the purchase of capital equipment from abroad most effectively, such controls of foreign trade would have to be combined with an appropriate internal fiscal policy. In any event, the probable need for priority ratings in the use of foreign exchange is a situation that must be taken into account when comprehensive international economic policies are developed.

This consideration is unimportant for a country like the United States, since we are fairly certain to have sufficient foreign exchange to meet all probable national wants for imported commodities. It is a paramount consideration for many countries, however, in choosing between greater or less national control of their foreign trade.

7. *National security often requires that a country maintain, through tariff protection or other national controls, industries whose products could be obtained more cheaply abroad.* Thus, as long as the danger of war exists, and as long as we are not assured of a wartime supply of natural rubber from abroad, we must maintain a sufficient domestic production of rubber to guard against disastrous consequences should our supplies from abroad once more be cut off. The validity of special protection of industries in the interest of national security has

been long recognized by economists. *The abuse of this argument to protect special interests has long been recognized also.*

8. Finally, the resumption of unregulated international trade has been rendered difficult because monetary and financial transactions cannot always be relied upon to reflect movements of actual goods and services. A serious problem, strengthening the case for retention of national exchange control, lies in the unpredictable international movements of "hot money." In the prewar period one of the most unsettling influences in international exchange markets was the swift, contagious, and often irrational flow of hot money from one financial center to another, especially from London to New York. The British in particular are apprehensive that, in the absence of effective control after the war, large quantities of hot money would again flow out of London, thus making it extremely difficult for Britain to maintain stability of the pound sterling. There is general agreement in all quarters in Britain that the government must be allowed to control so-called "capital movements" entailing the flow of hot money. As has been pointed out frequently, however, it would be difficult to carry out such control without supervising most other types of foreign-exchange transactions as well.

CONCLUSIONS

The advantages of international trade, discussed above, lead to the conclusion that its expansion during the postwar period is of great national importance. Consideration of the problems of such an expansion makes it evident that a policy that rested only on unilateral lowering of our trade barriers in the hope of reciprocal action by other countries would have scant prospect of success. Indeed, there is little chance that lowering of conventional trade barriers by all countries, although a very desirable part of a larger program, would, of itself, be adequate and permanently effective in expanding world trade. The quasi-automatic mechanisms of world trade, which functioned fairly successfully while international trade was a transaction between individuals, are no longer adequate when to a considerable degree such trade is between governments or between corporations or associations of corporations closely integrated with their respective governments.

The belief is growing that the only alternative to the continuance of national foreign trade controls is the development of coordinated international policies and programs and the creation of certain essential international economic institutions. Such institutions would in some degree replace national controls and to some extent set up working rules that limit the scope of national controls and prescribe the types of action permissible for such controls. The coordinated policies and programs of all countries, in part regulated and facilitated by the new types of international economic institutions and in part carried out by the separate governments themselves, must be directed first at releasing nations from the choice between domestic full employment and unregulated foreign trade, and second at inducing these nations to accept reciprocal limitations on methods of competition, essential to fair exchange in world markets. It is not easy to achieve both these aims while still preserving the degree of control over domestic economic affairs that each nation now demands. The principal elements of national and international policy and the requisite international institutions that seem to offer reasonably good prospects for achieving these ends are analyzed in the following chapters.

These chapters focus discussion upon the following subjects: (a) the problem of international currency stabilization and its proposed solution through the International Monetary Fund; (b) the problem of international loans and investments and the International Bank for Reconstruction and Development; (c) the newer forms of trade barriers and the growing importance of cartels; (d) our tariff policy; (e) our lend-lease policy; (f) our mercantile marine policy; (g) the problem of our new and overexpanded war industries; and (h) prospective trends in our foreign trade.

II. THE INTERNATIONAL
MONETARY FUND

I<small>N</small> <small>THE</small> International Monetary Fund, as set forth in the
document drawn up by delegates of forty-four nations
at the Bretton Woods Conference in July, 1944, we have a
fair sample of the problems of postwar international economic
cooperation and the type of compromise solution that may
result. It reflects the desire of the participating nations to
cooperate in the expansion of world trade and their recognition that present realities cannot be met by an attempted
return to the customs, policies, and procedures of 1914. It
represents an effort to substitute, at least partially, international control of foreign trade for national controls, and
also an attempt to reconcile a national wish to enjoy the
benefits of expanded world trade with the national will to
retain control of domestic affairs.

SOME IMPORTANT PROVISIONS OF THE
INTERNATIONAL MONETARY FUND

The guiding purposes of the International Monetary Fund
are stated in Art. I of the document proposing it:[1]

(i) To promote international monetary cooperation through a
permanent institution which provides the machinery for
consultation and collaboration on international monetary
problems.

(ii) To facilitate the expansion and balanced growth of international trade, and to contribute thereby to the promotion
and maintenance of high levels of employment and real

[1] United Nations Monetary and Financial Conference, Bretton Woods, N.H.,
July 1 to July 22, 1944, *Final Act and Related Documents*, Annex A, "Articles of
Agreement of the International Monetary Fund", U.S. Government Printing
Office, Washington, D.C., 1944, p. 28.

income and to the development of the productive resources of all members as primary objectives of economic policy.

(iii) To promote exchange stability, to maintain orderly exchange arrangements among members, and to avoid competitive exchange depreciation.

(iv) To assist in the establishment of a multilateral system of payments in respect of current transactions between members and in the elimination of foreign-exchange restrictions which hamper the growth of world trade.

(v) To give confidence to members by making the fund's resources available to them under adequate safeguards, thus providing them with opportunity to correct maladjustments in their balance of payments without resorting to measures destructive of national or international prosperity.

(vi) In accordance with the above, to shorten the duration and lessen the degree of disequilibrium in the international balance of payments of members.

The fund is to become effective when it has been accepted by governments representing at least 65 per cent of the total subscription but in no event before May 1, 1945. The agreement provides that each member nation shall have a quota, determining the amount of its subscription to the fund and its voting power.[1] Even more important, this quota determines what amount of its own currency a nation can sell to the fund to obtain other currencies. According to present accord, the United States is to subscribe $2,750 million, the United Kingdom $1,300 million, and Soviet Russia $1,200 million. Other countries are to subscribe smaller amounts, bringing the total fund to $8,800 million. The

[1] Note that the size of the quota is subject to change. The fund is empowered to review quotas every five years and to make adjustments that seem advisable. In addition, a member nation may apply at any time for an adjustment, subject to the approval of four-fifths of the fund's voting power. The original quotas were drawn up by means of a formula which took into consideration a country's national income, the prewar volume of its foreign trade, and its gold reserves. Political bargaining power was also a factor. The principal office of the fund is to be in the United States, since it has the largest quota.

agreement further stipulates that each country is to pay in gold 25 per cent of its quota or 10 per cent of its holdings of gold and United States dollars, whichever is smaller. The remainder of a country's subscription is to be paid in its own currency, or—at the fund's discretion—partially or totally in securities. In general, the voting power of the participating governments is in proportion to their quotas, although a rather complicated formula has been outlined to provide for variations from the strict ratio. Since the United States is to subscribe more than twice as much as any other country, its voting power is greater than that of any other member.

The proposed agreement provides further that the par value of each member's currency is to be expressed in terms of gold, as a common denominator, or in terms of the United States dollar of the weight and fineness in effect on July 1, 1944. The original par value of each member's currency shall be based on rates of exchange prevailing on the sixtieth day before the agreement goes into force.[1] In other words, in most cases the *de facto* rate of exchange is to be used as the initial rate for the purposes of the fund. Adjustments in initial par values are allowed, however, if the fund considers them necessary, within ninety days after the fund authorities

---

[1] Article XX, Sec. 4. "(*a*) When the fund is of the opinion that it will shortly be in a position to begin exchange transactions, it shall so notify the members and shall request each member to communicate within thirty days the par value of its currency based on the rates of exchange prevailing on the sixtieth day before the entry into force of this agreement. . . . (*b*) The par value communicated by a member whose metropolitan territory has not been occupied by the enemy shall be the par value of that member's currency for the purposes of this agreement unless, within ninety days after the request referred to in (*a*) above has been received, (i) the member notifies the fund that it regards the par value as unsatisfactory, or (ii) the fund notifies the member that in its opinion the par value cannot be maintained without causing recourse to the fund on the part of that member or others on a scale prejudicial to the fund and to the members. When notification is given under (i) or (ii) above, the fund and the member shall, within a period determined by the fund in the light of all relevant circumstances, agree upon a suitable par value for that currency. If the fund and the member do not agree within the period so determined, the member shall be deemed to have withdrawn from the fund on the date when the period expires."

first ask the member countries for their par values. Furthermore, a member nation may apply for a subsequent change in the par value of its currency in order to correct a "fundamental disequilibrium." When a member country proposes such a change, the fund shall first take into account any change already allowed in that country's initial par value, and if the proposed change together with all previous increases and decreases does not exceed 10 per cent of the initial par value, the fund "shall raise no objection." If the proposed change, plus all previous changes, does not exceed an additional 10 per cent of the original par value, the fund "may either concur or object," but it must make its decision within seventy-two hours if the member so requests. Should the proposed change, together with all previous changes, be greater than 20 per cent of the initial par value, the fund may either concur or object, but it shall be given a longer period to render judgment. The agreement provides that the fund shall concur in any proposed change "if it is satisfied that the change is necessary to correct a fundamental disequilibrium" and, in particular, that "it shall not object to a proposed change because of the domestic social or political policies of the member proposing the change." Lastly, should a member alter its par value despite the objection of the fund, the fund may declare such a country ineligible to use the fund's resources and may eventually force the member to withdraw from the organization.

The principal operations of the fund will be to supply any member (on the initiative of the member) with the currency of another member in exchange for gold or for the currency of the member desiring to make the purchase. To guard against exhausting the fund's supply of particular currencies, the agreement stipulates certain conditions under which a member may sell its currency to the fund: (*a*) The member must prove that the currency it wishes to purchase is needed for making payments that "are consistent with the provisions of this agreement." (*b*) The fund has not given notice that the desired currency is scarce. (*c*) The proposed transaction would not cause a total increase in the fund's holdings of the purchasing member's currency of more than 25 per cent of its quota during the year ending on the date of purchase. (This provision is to apply only if the fund's holdings after the transaction would exceed 75 per cent of the quota.)[1] Nor would the purchase cause the fund's holdings of the purchasing member's currency to exceed 200 per cent of the quota. (*d*) The member has not been declared ineligible to use the fund's resources.[2] It is later provided, however, that the fund may at its discretion, and "on terms which safeguard its interests," waive any of the above-mentioned conditions, "especially in the case of members with a record of avoiding large or continuous use of the fund's resources."[3]

The agreement contains important clauses concerning scarce currencies. It states that if a "general scarcity" of a particular currency is developing, the fund may so inform the members and may issue a report "setting forth the causes of the scarcity and containing recommendations designed to bring it to an end." Should the fund consider it necessary to replenish its holdings of the scarce currency, it may (*a*) propose that the member lend its currency to the fund (but the member is under no obligation to do so) or (*b*) require the member to sell its currency to the fund for gold. If, however, it becomes evident that "the demand for a member's cur-

---

[1] Article V, Sec. 8 provides for moderate penalty charges to be levied on the balance of a currency held by the fund in excess of the member's quota. However, these charges, graduated in relation to the excess, may not be an effective control in discouraging a member from making excess purchases.

[2] Article V, Sec. 5 gives the fund power to limit, and eventually refuse, the use of its resources by a member "using the resources of the fund in a manner contrary to the purposes of the fund."

[3] Article V, Sec. 4. "In making a waiver it [the fund] shall take into consideration periodic or exceptional requirements of the member requesting the waiver. The fund shall also take into consideration a member's willingness to pledge as collateral security gold, silver, securities, or other acceptable assets having a value sufficient in the opinion of the fund to protect its interests and may require as a condition of waiver the pledge of such collateral security."

rency seriously threatens the fund's ability to supply that currency," then the fund is empowered to *declare* such a currency scarce and to ration its existing supply "with due regard to the relative needs of members, the general international economic situation, and any other pertinent considerations."[1]

APPRAISAL OF THE FUND

The fund is designed to provide a mutual validation of the exchange values of the currencies of the participating countries. This is a step of utmost importance toward an early resumption of trade after the war. Though the problem of stabilizing the currencies for the long haul remains to be solved, there is immense advantage in having in the immediate postwar period temporary stabilization of almost all important currencies, making them acceptbale for the purchase of goods in any international market.

It has been argued justly that under the chaotic conditions that will exist immediately at the close of the war, the task of setting proper exchange rates for the various national currencies presents very grave difficulties.[2] It is further

[1] Article VII, Sec. 3 (*b*) provides that when the fund formally declares a particular currency scarce, any member, after consultation with the fund, has the right temporarily to impose restrictions on exchange operations in the scarce currency. The limitations must not be more stringent than is necessary to curb the demand for the scarce currency to the supply held by the member in question, and they are to be abandoned as soon as conditions permit.

[2] Some critics of the fund fear that member countries will desire dollars in such large amounts that the fund's resources will be quickly depleted. There is concern that under such circumstances countries unable to obtain dollars may blame the United States for being unwilling to make additional dollars available.

The supply of dollars would, however, obviously be larger if the fund were in existence than if it were not. It hardly seems likely that resentment over inability to obtain dollars under the regulations of the fund would be greater than if fewer dollars could be obtained because no fund existed.

It should be noted further that what amounts to mutual validation of the exchange values of national currencies tends to increase the total purchasing power in international trade of otherwise weak currencies, beyond the amounts made available through dollar advances by the fund. The advantages to international trade that would attend stable currencies as against weak and fluctuat-

argued that because some exchange rates may prove to have been set unwisely, the resources of the fund may be dissipated. On the other hand, it is certain that unstable currencies would prolong the period of political and economic instability in many countries. A beginning must be made sometime.

The "key countries" approach, by which in the beginning currencies of only a few major countries would be stabilized, is offered as an alternative to the fund. This method would have the distinct disadvantage of delaying the date when a permanent international institution could come to grips with the comprehensive problem.

The fund's validation of the exchange rates of the different currencies depends primarily upon what is, in effect, a loan from the United States, since United States currency will be more in demand than that of any other country. This is expected because of a great demand for our goods. Consequently, by contributing the sum of $2,750 million to the fund, we are virtually underwriting an export credit in that amount. Expressed in an oversimplified way, the United States government provides a guarantee that our exporters will be able to receive payment up to this amount for an excess of our exports over our imports. In the last analysis, we thus lend not gold and currency but the products of American industry and agriculture.[1]

The Bretton Woods agreement makes sharply evident the unlikelihood of a return to the 1914, or even to the 1929, system of largely unregulated international trade or to the

ing currencies (where these have limited availability or acceptability) differ only in degree from the general advantages to be had from a monetary medium of exchange as against direct barter of goods.

[1] This does not mean that the fund automatically authorizes the other members to use our contribution to the capital of the fund as a means of paying for imports from the United States. The uses of the fund's resources are controlled by substantial and particular limitations, intended to ensure that these resources are employed to meet temporary needs of members for maintaining their currencies at par. Still, since on balance there will probably be a stronger demand for United States dollars than for other currencies, the net effect is that of an export credit.

gold standard, so closely associated with it.[1]   Instead, it is an augury of the willingness of the nations to cooperate in international institutions, intended, first, to facilitate international exchange of goods and services through elimination of bilateralism and through return to multilateralism and, second, to enable the nations by reciprocal renunciation to dispense with some of the national controls of foreign trade, which had developed mainly during and after the great depression of the 1930's.[2]   This agreement reflects a readiness to agree upon a set of working rules limiting the scope and the methods of the national controls that are retained.

It is of the utmost significance that, during the discussions leading up to the Bretton Woods Conference and at the actual negotiations, Great Britain, long the "executive secretary" for the gold standard and the high priestess of free

---

[1] Lord Keynes had to assure what was apparently a great majority of the British Parliament that there would be no return to the automatic gold standard. Lord Keynes himself was, in fact, very much opposed to a return to the gold standard.   It should be noted, however, that the United States and Britain, one the largest holder and the other the largest producer of gold, have seen to it that the fund contributes to a strong market for gold.   For example, the agreement provides not only that the par value of each member's currency shall be defined in gold [Art. IV, Sec. 1 (a)], but also that no member shall buy gold at a price above par value plus a margin prescribed by the fund or sell gold at a price below par value minus a similar margin (Art. IV, Sec. 2).   It is also stipulated that a member may purchase with gold from the fund any currency it may desire [Art. V, Sec. 6 (a)], and that the fund may buy scarce currencies with gold (Art. VII, Sec. 2).   Also, nothing in the agreement prevents any member from selling newly produced gold in any market [Art. V, Sec. 6 (b)].

[2] Despite the ultimate aim to eliminate national controls, the agreement provides that in the postwar transitional period member countries "may maintain and adapt to changing circumstances restrictions on payments and transfers for current international transactions" (Art. XIV).   Members should remove such restrictions as soon as possible, however, and particularly as soon as they are convinced that they will be able without such restrictions "to settle their balance of payments in a manner which will not unduly encumber their access to the resources of the fund."   Five years after the beginning of the fund, those members still retaining restrictions on current exchange transactions must consult annually with the fund concerning their restrictions, and the fund may make suggestions for the elimination of these restraints.   An uncooperative member is subject to expulsion from the fund.

international trade, should have taken the leadership among those concerned lest measures to restore a greater freedom of trade in the world should, in practice, operate to limit the power of national governments to control their domestic economic policies. The British have made it abundantly clear that they intend to carry out a program of domestic full employment even if this means retention of exchange control and other national controls and barriers to the free movement of international trade.[1] The British are fearful that should they return to old-style international trade or to a new system operating in a similar fashion, they might face so large a deficit in their international balance of payments that deflationary measures would be unavoidable to restore the balance. Thus, if the International Monetary Fund or some similar mechanism did not exist, a system of fixed exchange rates between the pound and other currencies, without exchange control or import quotas, might make impossible the maintenance of a high rate of employment in British industry.

The British situation, like that of several other countries whose economies have been seriously affected by the war, will be particularly difficult in the immediate postwar period. The high level of employment, which these countries are determined to maintain, will create a high level of consumer income. This, in turn, will cause a large demand for consumer goods of all kinds, including those imported from abroad. However, the increase in demand for imported consumer goods will coincide with the need for large amounts of imported raw materials and capital equipment required to repair the ravages of war, to replenish exhausted inventories,

[1] In view of Britain's great fear of a renewal of the flow of hot money from London at the end of the war, it is interesting to note that Art. VI provides that a member may not make "net use of the fund's resources to meet a large and sustained outflow of capital," and that a member may be requested "to exercise controls to prevent such a use of the resources of the fund." In addition, "members may exercise such controls as are necessary to regulate capital movements. . . . " (Sec. 3.)

and to replace depreciated equipment. If these countries were to obtain the essential raw materials and the capital equipment from each other, no difficulty in payment need arise, since imports and exports would tend to balance each other. If, however, these commodities must be obtained from countries that are not importing equivalent amounts of goods and services, potential difficulties in payment will appear promptly.

These difficulties in paying for imports can be temporarily overcome if the supplier countries extend sufficient credit or loans for this purpose. During the immediate postwar period these loans will be almost a necessity, regardless of other means employed to resolve the problem. If the Bretton Woods plans are adopted, the International Monetary Fund and the International Bank for Reconstruction and Development will provide a good part of the resources required for this. However, these, or indeed any loans and credit, would be but partial and temporary solutions.

If countries in the position of Great Britain were to find that they continue to incur large deficits in their balance of payments, they would have to take direct steps to restore their international balance of payments. This might be done through deflationary or anti-inflationary measures, such as fiscal measures designed to balance the national budget, including the raising of taxes and the curtailing of governmental expenditures. Such measures would be more comprehensive and effective if they included lowering wages, raising interest rates, curtailing bank credit and commercial credit, and compulsory reduction in inventories. But such steps would inevitably cause widespread unemployment. The combination of unemployment with other unpopular deflationary measures would not be tolerated for long by the people of a democracy; no government could pursue such policies and stay in office.

Since deflationary measures on a scale that would be effective in bringing about equilibrium in the importing country's balance of payments are excluded, two other alternatives remain. These are devaluation of the currency and the resumption of direct control of foreign trade through exchange control, import quotas, and like measures. Through exchange control and related measures, a country could limit the importing of certain types of goods considered non-essential from the standpoint of the national economy, thereby reserving the stock of foreign exchange for raw materials and essential commodities. A further step would be to limit, by exchange control and associated measures, the importation of certain goods from specific countries with whom the balance of payments was strongly in deficit. Devaluation of the currency could also discourage imports and encourage exports, and this, for a time at least, would tend to correct the imbalance of international payments for the importing country.

In setting up the International Monetary Fund, Britain and the countries supporting the British position have taken great care to embody in the document all the alternatives to deflationary action. Effective provisions stipulate that exchange control need not be abolished until the period of the war emergency has passed.[1] The agreement provides that virtual exchange control and associated measures can be reinstituted with the assent of the fund if the situation renders this necessary. National currencies can also be devalued under rather liberal provisions,[2] and the management of the fund cannot deny on account of political or social considerations[3] a request for permission to devalue a national currency.

The fund purports to be a real stride toward stabilizing international exchange rates and eliminating national exchange controls, while at the same time it accepts condi-

[1] See footnote 2, p. 41.

[2] See above, pp. 34–39.

[3] The question at once arises whether a request for devaluation might be refused by the fund because of a country's failure to balance its budget in combination with a program of full employment. It appears likely that such a reason would be excluded from consideration as being at least quasi-political and social.

tions under which exchange rates of currencies may be altered and national exchange controls reinstituted. Is not this duality illogical? It may not be logical but it is the type of compromise that must be accepted if any alternative to complete national control of foreign trade is to be forthcoming. The compromise does permit the retention of some national control of foreign trade at all times; it allows an increase in the scope of such control under some circumstances; it leaves the way open for departures from previously agreed upon values for national currencies. All these are made possible through a series of escape clauses.[1]

Such a compromise, implemented by escape clauses, has immense advantages. First, it introduces a measure of order into the operations of national foreign trade controls. It provides for international notice of intention before a country resorts to increased national controls of foreign trade. It enables the nations to try out the substitution of international control for national controls of foreign trade, while affording a means of escape from international obligations and institutions if they prove unworkable or onerous, without the accompaniment of recriminations and bitterness.[2]

Although the assurance that the fund will not compel a member country to resort to deflationary measures entails obvious dangers, it still possesses material advantages to the other members. Hard experience has taught us that an economic depression in an important country is almost certain to spread to other nations unless the most strenuous measures are taken to isolate the afflicted country's economy. The existence of the fund constitutes a strong guarantee that a member country will not *suddenly* have to resort to deflationary measures that might seriously disturb international economic

[1] Although the fund does not prevent the use of tariffs, quotas, monopolies of foreign trade, or, indeed, various other barriers to, or controls of, foreign trade, the adoption of the fund plan, which is a form of compromise between the retention of national controls of foreign trade and an unobstructed international trade, does facilitate the latter.

[2] In the last analysis a member may withdraw from the fund (Art. XVI).

confidence. It affords the possibility for a country, where expansion in business activity and monetary national income have surpassed the capacity to produce real national income, to take corrective measures gradually which, if introduced suddenly and rigorously would be almost certain to produce an economic depression.

It is true that the powers of the fund appear insufficient to compel a member country to take such salutary but always distasteful remedies. On this point, national economic sovereignty was preserved at the expense of international authority. It seems fairly clear that while the fund contains adequate guarantees that its powers will not be used to compel any country to undertake unreasonably deflationary measures, it does not contain comparable assurances against the use of its powers and facilities for inflationary purposes.

On the other hand, the existence of the fund would not increase the danger of inflation above that which would exist if only national controls of foreign trade were to continue; indeed, under some circumstances it would lessen the danger of inflation. The funds that debtor countries may obtain to meet temporarily adverse balances of payments are not large in relation to their potential adverse balances of payment. Presumably, such funds will be used mainly to meet deficits arising out of the purchase of raw materials and capital equipment to enlarge domestic production. The tendency toward a rising price level in the deficit country would be abated to this extent. However, the export of goods by a country such as the United States, by means of credit furnished by it through the fund to an importing country, might indeed produce a potentially inflationary effect in this country, since it would have somewhat the same consequences as a general subsidy of exports. However, such inflationary effect would be offset to the extent that resources otherwise idle were used to produce the additional exports.[1] Likewise, the amount of

[1] It is important to note that under conditions of unemployed resources, and with the operation of the "multiplier effect," the provision of such funds might

credit available from this source in any one year is almost certainly not large enough in itself to produce any strongly inflationary results.

No one can foretell the success or failure of this first comprehensive effort to set up an international monetary institution aimed at effecting a compromise between national sovereignty over the domestic economy and some degree of international control over foreign trade. There can be hardly any doubt that present-day national controls of the domestic economy constitute serious limitations on the automatic operation of international trade, which before 1914 provided a kind of equilibrium in the international balance of payments.[1] One cannot be certain whether or not the creation of new types of international regulatory institutions, of which the International Monetary Fund and the International Bank for Reconstruction and Development are the initial examples, will resolve the conflict of interest and power. However, the existence of this potential conflict was fully recognized by the delegates to the Bretton Woods Conference. The document shows remarkable skill in drafting the agreement so as to minimize the problem.

It is apparent that the delegates to the conference were well aware that the fund would not be able to stand by itself. The same conference therefore produced a document setting up the International Bank for Reconstruction and Development.[2] Unquestionably, the resources of the bank are counted upon to take some of the pressure for advances off

---

be costless to the American economy. In the same way and under similar circumstances, a domestic program of public works or an extension of our social-insurance program could be fundamentally costless.

[1] See, on this point, John H. Williams, "Currency Stabilization: The Keynes and White Plans," *Foreign Affairs*, July, 1943, and "Currency Stabilization: American and British Attitudes," *ibid.*, January, 1944. An unpublished paper by Gardiner C. Means also develops the difficulties in achieving equilibrium in the international balance of payments under conditions of "rigid" domestic prices and fixed rates of exchange between national currencies.

[2] See Chap. III for a discussion of the International Bank for Reconstruction and Development.

the fund, and thus aid it in meeting the demand for scarce currencies, particularly United States dollars.

It is equally apparent that the establishment of the fund and of the bank was intended to be only the first step in a general program for the revival and expansion of world trade, which is to include lowering of tariffs and removal of import quotas as well as the progressive relaxation of exchange controls and associated measures.

The fund seems to have staked its future largely on the success of the measures to achieve full employment in the major participating countries. Prolonged depression in any one of these countries would jeopardize the position of the fund, initiating a new wave of capital flights, currency devaluations, and exchange restrictions. The very existence of the fund, however, is counted upon to prevent depressions from gaining headway, since it goes a long way to ward off the necessity for deflationary measures by participating countries in temporary financial difficulties.

Conditions of full employment are counted upon to create a favorable climate for the removal of tariffs and other trade barriers. Above all, full employment[1] is relied upon to increase immensely the need for goods and services, and particularly American requirements for raw materials, so that the dilemma of unbalanced demand on the fund for United States dollars may be resolved.[2]

[1] The term "full employment" is used in the sense in which economists all over the world now employ it. That is, full employment does not mean that everyone would be actually employed. Neither does it mean that everyone who wanted a job would be able to obtain one at once. In a country the size of the United States, for example, there is in peacetime a more or less irreducible minimum of several million unemployed, consisting of the seasonally unemployed, those who have voluntarily left employment and are seeking more desirable jobs, and those temporarily unemployed because of the loss of markets by particular industries and firms and for similar frictional reasons. In addition, there always will be a number of persons in the no man's land between being employable and being unemployable because of mental or physical handicaps. Thus, "full employment" simply connotes freedom from unemployment caused by economic depression.

[2] Our demand for raw materials would aid European countries that had a

The services the fund would render to an early revival of orderly international trade would seem to justify our participation in it. Moreover, the fund would forestall international ill feeling that may arise if currencies were to remain entirely unstabilized during the postwar period. We hardly can afford to forego the opportunity the fund would provide for the launching of synchronized national strategies to achieve full employment, with their favorable effect upon international entrepreneurial expectations.

No doubt there are features of the agreement setting up the fund that could be changed so that they would favor our national interests more. No doubt technical improvements could be made in the scheme for the fund's operation. It seems unlikely, however, that a better plan could be developed and adopted if this one were discarded. If the United States or any other major country should not ratify the agreement, the most significant of the initial steps toward revival of international trade on a basis of current realities would consequently fail and the prospects for relaxation of national controls of foreign trade would not be bright. Consequently, the case for ratification by the United States of the agreement establishing the fund is very strong.[1]

---

deficit in their balance of payments with us, since our non-European suppliers of raw materials would increase their demand for European manufactured goods. They would pay for increased amounts of these goods with the dollar exchange earned from the sale of raw materials to the United States.

[1] Advocacy of the fund and the bank as set forth in these pages may be in some degree inconsistent with the position that large and continuous government loans to maintain a heavy export surplus would be decidedly inadvisable. Advocacy of the fund and the bank is based upon the belief that the proposed capital contributions by the United States government are not unreasonably large for setting up the essential international monetary mechanism that would give an initial impulse to world trade and investment and would provide a means of continuously facilitating them. If adherence to the fund and bank meant the necessity for continuing large additions to the capital resources of the two institutions, such adherence would not appear to be in the national interest.

III. THE PROBLEM OF INTERNATIONAL LOANS AND INVESTMENTS: THE INTERNATIONAL BANK FOR RECONSTRUCTION AND DEVELOPMENT

THE GENERAL PROBLEM

BETWEEN World War I and World War II the United States was in a creditor position on long-term account. This condition was closely related to a strong tendency toward a continuously active balance of payments. Not only did we have a large export surplus in goods, but the imports represented in foreign shipping services, services to American tourists traveling abroad, and so forth, were insufficient to offset the export surplus of commodities. Total payments due the United States by other countries for goods and services sent currently or in the past to these countries tended to be greater than similar payments due by Americans to foreigners. With the depression of the early 1930's, however, this tendency was retarded by exchange controls, import quotas, and other measures adopted by foreign governments, aimed to diminish the deficits in their balances of payments through restrictions on imports—which often operated particularly to curtail imports from the United States.

Our prewar tendency toward an export surplus of commodities will be accentuated in the postwar years by the fact that we shall emerge from the war with our capacity to produce goods for export not only substantially unimpaired but greatly expanded. In this respect we shall be better off than any other important manufacturing country, with the possible exceptions of Canada and Sweden. While the British capacity to produce goods for export will be about the same as before the war,[1] large imports of raw materials will be needed for their industries as well as great supplies of lumber and other materials to rebuild their bombed cities.

It will be several years before the productive capacity of Germany and Japan can be restored, even if the peace terms permit restoration of their industries to something like their prewar condition. In varying degrees Russia, Poland, Italy, Norway, and France, and perhaps Czechoslovakia also will be confronted with problems of rebuilding war-shattered industries. In the first postwar years these countries and the nations they formerly supplied with manufactured goods will turn to the United States, Great Britain, Canada, and Sweden for much of their needed imports.

British foreign investments, upon which the United Kingdom relied heavily in maintaining a balance in her international payments, have been seriously depleted during the war.[2] A substantial portion of Britain's assets in the United States and in other parts of the world have been liquidated to

[1] In some fields the efficiency of British industry probably has been increased through retooling made possible by lend-lease.

[2] The British journal, *The Economist*, in its issue of January 8, 1944, estimates the British balance of payments in the three years before the war as follows:

BALANCE OF PAYMENTS OF THE UNITED KINGDOM, 1936–1938
(Figures are the average of the three years in millions of pounds sterling)

Debit		Credit	
Imports	930	Exports	540
Government payments	10	Investment income	200
		Shipping earnings	110
		Commissions, etc	40
		Other receipts	10
			900
		Deficit	40
	940		940

The Economist comments: "The immediate effect of the war will be to reduce very severely the 'invisible' items on the credit side. Even if there were no other elements in the problem it is probable that there would be a gap (including the prewar deficit) of at least £200 million on the credit side." It then concludes that, all things considered, the British must increase their exports by 50 per cent in the postwar period if a neutral balance of payments is to be achieved.

help finance the war. Moreover, she has an enormous blocked sterling debt to India and other countries of the sterling area. And her investments in the territories lost to Japan will have declined severely in value by the time they are restored to her.

The United Kingdom's competitive position as a carrier of the world's merchandise—always one of her great assets—will have been impaired by her loss of merchant shipping and by the construction of a huge American merchant marine. Insofar as American synthetic rubber replaces imports of crude rubber, new processes of tin plating and tin-plate substitutes reduce American imports of tin, and nylon and other synthetic fibers replace silk, the surplus in our balance of payments will tend to increase. It seems probable, therefore, that the postwar trend in the international balance of payments will produce an active balance for the United States in relation to the aggregate of countries trading with it.[1]

While it seems most likely that a surplus in exports by the United States will continue after the war, it appears that our creditor-debtor status has undergone a change during the war. If all debts owed the United States government or its nationals by foreign governments or their nationals were valued at their face amounts, the United States would enter the postwar period as a creditor on a huge scale. In actual fact most of these debts have little or no part in determining the debtor-creditor status of the United States in the postwar world. This is true, of course, of all war debts that remain from World War I and of most of the debts that were defaulted or had their servicing stopped by national exchange controls during the 1930's. Certainly the major portion of our lend-lease loans could not be collected even if we wished to do so.

By contrast, gold and foreign-exchange resources of a considerable number of foreign countries have increased appreci-

---

[1] From a long-run viewpoint, the wartime depletion of our deposits of high-grade iron ore, copper, zinc, lead, bauxite, and petroleum will partly offset our tendency toward a "favorable" balance of payments.

ably. This is true of Sweden, Switzerland, Portugal, Turkey, Spain, Egypt, Iran, India, and of most of the Latin American countries.[1] It applies in some degree to Belgium, the Netherlands, and Norway. Consequently, we appear in a net debtor position with respect to most of these countries on short-term account. These increases in gold or foreign exchange resulted from payments by the United States and Great Britain for ordinary imports of goods and services, for troops quartered in these countries, for strategic materials for direct and indirect military use, and the construction of ports, roads, and airports. The payments had to be made in gold or foreign exchange rather than through exports of goods and services because of war limitations on production and shipping. Ultimately, the bulk of these sums had to be furnished by the United States, since British resources were insufficient for the purpose.[2]

The British have incurred a huge indebtedness in blocked sterling, estimated at $12 billion. This is owed primarily to countries of the sterling area, notably India. These funds cannot be employed to purchase goods outside the United Kingdom and, indeed, cannot buy goods even in the United Kingdom during the war, and perhaps for some time after, since the British have neither stocks of goods nor current production from which purchases could be made. The liquidation of these balances represents one of the most pressing problems for the British and their creditors.

[1] Great Britain as well as the United States has contributed heavily to the foreign-exchange resources of these countries.

[2] One estimate places the gold and dollar holdings of foreign countries at the end of September, 1944, at around $17 billion, compared with $7 billion or $8 billion at the close of the 1920's (*Federal Reserve Bulletin*, November, 1944).

According to another estimate (*News Letter of the National City Bank of New York*, August, 1944) aggregate foreign-owned gold and dollar balances, including foreign-owned banking funds in the United States but not foreign-owned American securities or direct investments, amounted to about $22 billion. By contrast, total foreign-owned gold and short-term dollar balances amounted to only $5 billion in 1919. This estimate of current resources may be too high, but the fact that gold holdings and dollar resources are large is unquestionable.

The dollar balances and gold holdings of a number of countries appear large enough to ensure strong demand for American exports immediately on cessation of hostilities and for some time thereafter. A long-continuing American export surplus, however, would constitute a most serious problem. If, after the war, the balance of payments is "in our favor" by several billion dollars a year, the net surplus of goods and services sold by the United States would have to be paid for in one or a combination of the following ways: (*a*) the absorption of dollar balances and gold holdings accumulated during the war by such countries as Sweden, Switzerland, Portugal, and the Latin American nations, as well as similar resources remaining from the prewar period, as in the case of France; (*b*) the extension of short-term commercial or government credits; (*c*) the granting of loans by our government or by our nationals; or (*d*) the growth of direct American investments abroad.[1]

Should our active balance of payments be greater than the total of existing dollar balances and gold holdings plus credits, loans, and investments extended by the United States to foreign countries, pressure against the currencies of countries having a passive balance of payments would be inevitable. A seriously passive trade balance in Great Britain, unless covered by loans or credit, would mean a depreciation of sterling in terms of the dollar. If the trend were to continue unchanged, the British probably would resort to exchange control, import quotas, or other trade restrictions, all likely to involve discrimination against the United States. Under these controls, only commodities essential to the economic life of Great Britain would be purchased abroad. Rationing their scarce foreign exchange, priority would be given to purchases of basic raw materials

[1] In actual fact, the most urgent need for loans and credits during the years immediately after the war may be expected in Great Britain, Soviet Russia, the Balkan countries, and China (in addition to the defeated Axis powers), since most other countries will probably be able to finance their immediate needs from existing gold and foreign-exchange resources.

and food, and funds for other imports would be granted only when the supply of foreign exchange was not exhausted by the essential purchases.

For a time, all the difficulties outlined above can be averted if our new credits, loans, and investments abroad are as large as our export surplus of goods and services. Indeed, the volume of our credits, loans, and investments abroad may be the dynamic factor; the larger this total, the greater our exports of goods and services. The world apparently stands ready to take a tremendous volume of American exports if sufficient funds are provided either by American loans or by increase of American imports.

Unfortunate past experience with foreign loans and investments may be a serious deterrent to the movement of private American capital abroad. This experience has ranged from outright repudiation and expropriation, as in Russia after the revolution, and practical expropriation, as in Manchuria after the Japanese occupation, to partial expropriation via exchange controls that blocked the payments of funds to foreigners, as in Germany. The American experience, moreover, has been pretty much that of all foreign investors.

This increased insecurity of foreign loans and investments is caused only partially by maladjustments in foreign trade and finance. Some of it is due to a rising tide of nationalism in countries that have attracted foreign capital, and an antagonism to capitalism and to capitalists in general. In Russia, for example, the property of both native and foreign capitalists was expropriated. Wherever social revolutionary movements develop, the foreign capitalist, however, is usually disliked more than the native capitalist, and his investments are often the first to fall victim to the revolutionary sentiment.

The full impact of partial expropriations through exchange control and blocked accounts has been obscured somewhat by the fact that a portion of the short-term loans by Americans was recouped. The very large gold shipments to the United States after 1932 helped to liquidate a considerable part of the

American investment abroad. It is essential to remember, however, that the gold we have received in such vast amounts since 1914 has been practically useless for normal peacetime purposes even though our gold holdings have been of some worth as a war chest. Our gold imports were not directly a balancing item against our net current surplus of exports; they represented mainly the liquidation of our foreign investments (partly made possible by previous export surpluses) and the transfer of foreign-owned funds to the United States. It is somewhat ironical that foreign funds were being transferred and invested in the United States during a period when even the interest and dividends on a large portion of American investments abroad could not be realized.

Not all the funds transferred by foreigners have been invested after reaching this country; much of the capital has been held in liquid balances. The gold transfer is often referred to as "a great movement of capital to the United States." Such a view is superficial and misleading. *This movement of gold to the United States did not, on balance, add anything tangible to our capital goods and equipment.* In recent years the process has amounted to the United States government's issuing money or bank credit in return for the imported gold (though the exact technical process was somewhat different). While there were many unemployed men and machines in the United States, this produced no harmful results. Indeed it probably made the expansion of bank credit and of employment considerably easier politically for the Roosevelt administration. *There was no fundamental reason, however, why issuance of paper currency or the expansion of our money and credit system should have been related to the quantity of gold that persons happened to want to bring into this country.* As a nation, in effect, we gave away participating shares in our industry in return for metal that is of use only if sometime we can induce other countries to accept it in return for useful goods and services.[1]

[1] This problem of gold movements is closely connected with that of capital movements. It seems probable that, even if an international banking and

Even when loans and investments abroad are maintained at a rate to match any excess of exports over imports, a serious problem is bound to arise should this process continue on a large scale indefinitely. Any attempt to realize on foreign credits, loans, and investments (as happened at the beginning of the depression) would produce a crisis; were sudden crises avoided, the borrowing countries still would have to cope with a steadily increasing burden of interest and dividend payments. *Of course, the problem would vanish were the process reversed someday, with the lending country accepting the repayment of interest and dividends in the form of an excess of imports of goods and services.* Actually, it did work out very much this way in the case of Great Britain and her debtors. For some years Great Britain has been able to pay for an excess of commodity imports partially out of income from investments abroad. The British difficulty was not her unwillingness to accept goods in payment of interest and dividends but the insolvency or recalcitrance of some of the borrowers.

There seem to be no dependable, inherent laws, however, which guarantee that at the appropriate moment a country will cease to be an exporter of capital and become a *rentier* nation. If it fails to achieve this, and if the export surplus continues indefinitely, the amount of its investments will snowball through reinvestment of interest and dividends. Ultimately this process breaks down and precipitates a crisis. Countries with passive balances of payments will then institute exchange control or import quotas, and thereby the lender's export surplus, which underwrote the extension of credits, loans, and investments, will be curtailed. The

---

currency system were adopted with the purpose of eventually eliminating exchange control, capital movements, both inward and outward, would be controlled by most countries (as the International Monetary Fund provides) and that gold movements might likewise be restricted. It seems questionable whether we should be willing to accept indefinitely what amounts to gold "poker chips" that we never may wish to redeem and that might not be accepted by other countries in payment for real values should we ever wish to "cash them in."

antagonism nations often feel toward foreigners holding large investments in their economy greatly facilitates the institution of exchange control, which blocks the payment of interest and dividends on foreign loans and investments.

The conclusion from the foregoing is that a national policy in international trade and finance based upon the assumption of a constant and heavy export surplus and large and continuous loans and investments abroad is not likely to be in the ultimate national interest.

That excessive loans by government, or private loans or credit guaranteed by government, may interfere with the free development of domestic production as well as foreign trade should not be overlooked.[1] Distortions of this sort are usually hidden by the complex industrial pattern of a nation. They would be apparent in the case of a carelessly administered and generous policy of credit guarantees to exporters of goods shipped to particular countries. In effect, such credits might amount to export subsidies. The displacements they would introduce into our domestic production would be the reverse of a protective tariff. The effect upon our trade relations with competing nations would be much the same as that of outright export subsidies.

Still, as long as we do export a surplus of goods and services, we must extend credits and loans or invest abroad if we wish such an export surplus to continue. Since there is a limit to the amount of short-term credit that will be extended, long-term investment and loans would have to be made to ward off a crisis.

It appears desirable, however, to prevent this export surplus

---

[1] This danger is probably greater in the case of loans by government than may be true of loans by private capital. If government-guaranteed loans are made as part of a "make work" policy accompanied by deficit spending, the temptation to pay small attention to the safety of principal and interest is likely to be strong. This argument does not run in any important degree against the International Bank for Reconstruction and Development, because it is unlikely that its loans would be tied up with work-creation plans of any particular national government, and because the provisions to assure repayment seem reasonably adequate.

from becoming unwieldy and chronic. This can be accomplished in part by accepting more goods and services. Lowering our own protective tariff offers one means of increasing the volume of our imports in relation to our exports.

No matter how important the changes we make in our tariff policy, aimed at increasing our imports, the avoidance of deflation and the maintenance of full employment within the United States are more important. The volume of our imports seems to be affected primarily by changes in industrial activity and in national income in the United States. Thus, an increase of $10 billion in gross national product may be expected to increase imports by, say, half a billion dollars. Exports also tend to be increased by an expansion in industrial activity; but this is largely a reflection of increased dollar exchange made available through increased imports. Of course, the effect of expanded employment and production in the United States upon our net import-export balance depends also on prevailing business conditions in the principal countries with which we trade. In any event, a high level of national prosperity in the United States is likely to increase our imports relative to our exports.

Greater attention should be paid to other potential means of altering the operation of our economy to prevent the existence either of export surpluses or investment surpluses on a scale that would disrupt our internal economy or our international trade. Funds for investment abroad comprise part of the total supply of investment funds. In the typical modern capitalistic economy the amount of capital funds that actually can come into existence and be invested depends upon the size of the national income but is limited by the opportunities for investment. During periods of less than full employment much larger funds for both investment and/or consumption would come into existence were there more opportunities for investment and greater effective consumption demand. Export surpluses have constituted a temporary escape from this dilemma. Goods are often marketed abroad even when the net return is less than is being currently received in the domestic market, since they can be shunted to foreign markets without lowering the price on the internal market. An export surplus arising in this way makes initial investments and loans abroad possible, but it is likely to be attended by resistance to the acceptance of the imports eventually necessary to service these loans and investments.[1]

A policy which combined measures to achieve full employment with measures to increase the proportion of national income received by persons in the lower income brackets would enlarge the proportion of the national income consumed at home. This would probably forestall a chronic export-surplus problem[2] and might help to avoid the crisis always impending if there is continuous lending and investing abroad and if there is any interruption in the stream of loans.

The amount of purely private loans and investments made in foreign countries by our citizens almost certainly will not be enough to provide for the maintenance of our potential surplus of exports over imports during the first years after the war.[3] In spite of the undesirability of an indefinitely prolonged export surplus, its existence for several years seems almost inevitable and even desirable. To the extent that such an export surplus consisted of "excess" domestic goods, and if we could not otherwise provide demand for the labor

---

[1] As long as unemployed economic factors exist, an export surplus approximates an international lend-lease which, in a certain sense, is costless. In effect, it is the same thing as a domestic WPA or FERA except that foreign countries get the bridges, buildings, and "surplus" commodities.

[2] In practice this presents serious difficulties. Measures aimed at the redistribution of income should seek to spare incentives to invest.

[3] There is some logical difficulty in so stating the matter, since the amount of our exports will actually depend, at least in part, upon how much we lend and invest abroad. If loans and investments are at a minimum, our exports probably will tend to be reduced through the operation of exchange controls and import quotas after the first seller's-market period has passed and after inventories and production facilities have been restored abroad. If a greater volume of loans and investments were made, the volume of our exports would probably increase proportionately.

used, we should be able to make an almost costless contribution to international reconstruction and development. Such a situation might arise in the aluminum, magnesium, machine-tool, and aviation industries. These industries and the men employed in them would benefit from action that permitted the maintenance of a larger export surplus than would otherwise exist.

It is desirable that as large a proportion as possible of our private investments abroad should be of the equity type. Direct investment, through stock ownership or through the establishment of branch plants abroad, is less likely to be withdrawn suddenly and it does not come due at some definite date when the international economic situation may or may not be favorable for the payment and transfer of funds. On the other hand, the advantages of equity-type investment are sometimes overstated. Though investments in stocks or outright ownership do not come due, the decision of owners to sell such investments might put pressure on a weak currency exactly as if bonds were to mature. Furthermore, even if business conditions are bad, particular companies may declare dividends, which may be just as difficult to transfer as if interest on bonds were involved.

Direct investment does have an advantage in that it is often accompanied by one of the most useful forms of international export, namely, the export of know-how of engineering and managerial skill. There is every reason why the whole world should share in our advanced industrial and agricultural technique, and its association with capital investment in foreign countries might diminish the antagonism so often attending such investment.

THE INTERNATIONAL BANK
FOR RECONSTRUCTION AND DEVELOPMENT

The International Bank for Reconstruction and Development, agreed upon at the Bretton Woods Conference, seems admirably designed to facilitate private investment of American capital abroad under governmental guarantee, guidance, and regulation.[1] The agreement also provides for direct loans by the bank. The purposes of the bank, by which it is to be guided in all its decisions, are as follows:

(i) To assist in the reconstruction and development of territories of members by facilitating the investment of capital for productive purposes, including the restoration of economies destroyed or disrupted by war, the reconversion of productive facilities to peacetime needs and the encouragement of the development of productive facilities and resources in less developed countries.

(ii) To promote private foreign investment by means of guarantees or participations in loans and other investments made by private investors; and when private capital is not available on reasonable terms, to supplement private investment by providing, on suitable conditions, finance for productive purposes out of its own capital, funds raised by it, and its other resources.

(iii) To promote the long-range balanced growth of international trade and the maintenance of equilibrium in balances of payments by encouraging international investments for the development of the productive resources of members, thereby assisting in raising productivity, the standard of living, and conditions of labor in their territories.

(iv) To arrange the loans made or guaranteed by it in relation to international loans through other channels so that the more useful and urgent projects, large and small alike, will be dealt with first.

(v) To conduct its operations with due regard to the effect of international investment on business conditions in the

---

[1] The agreement setting up the bank must be ratified by the governments of the participating countries before it becomes binding upon any one country. It will enter into force when it has been signed by governments representing no less than 65 per cent of the total capital subscriptions, but in no event will it go into effect before May 1, 1945 (United Nations Monetary and Financial Conference, Bretton Woods, N.H., July 1 to July 22, 1944, *Final Act and Related Documents*, Annex B, "Articles of Agreement of the International Bank for Reconstruction and Development," Art. XI, Sec. 1, pp. 68–69).

territories of members and, in the immediate postwar years, to assist in bringing about a smooth transition from a wartime to a peacetime economy.

The basic power for management of the bank is provided through the appointment by each member country of one governor, whose voting power is to be in rough proportion to the capital subscribed by the respective nation. There are to be twelve executive directors to whom the board of governors may delegate all but certain reserved powers.[1] The directors are responsible for conducting the general operations of the bank. One director is to be appointed by each of the five member governments having the largest amounts of subscribed capital, and the remaining seven are to be elected by the other member governments. A total capital of $10 billion is authorized,[2] of which $9.1 billion has been allocated to countries represented at the conference. In general, the capital subscription of each country is of the same magnitude as its quota in the International Monetary Fund. The agreement provides that the capital stock may be increased by a three-fourths majority of the voting power when the bank deems it advisable. Only 20 per cent of a country's capital subscription must be paid at the beginning, the remaining 80 per cent being subject to call.[3] Only 2 per cent of each nation's capital subscription is payable in gold or United States dollars, the remaining 18 per cent being payable in the currency of the member country. In case of a call for any portion of the additional 80 per cent, payment may be made

---

[1] For example, the board of governors may not delegate its powers to admit new members, increase or decrease the capital stock, or suspend a member. See Art. V, Sec. 2.

[2] The capital stock is divided into 100,000 shares, each having a par value of $100,000 (Art. II, Sec. 2). The subscriptions to the capital of the bank are: United States, $3,175 million; United Kingdom, $1,300 million; Soviet Russia, $1,200 million; China, $600 million; France, $450 million. The principal office of the bank is to be in the United States, since it has been allotted the largest subscription to the stock of the bank.

[3] For the provisions regarding the payment of subscriptions, see Art. II, Sec. 7.

in gold, in United States dollars, or in the currency required to meet the bank's obligations.

Only 20 per cent of the bank's resources may be used for financing its direct loans. It may guarantee loans by private individuals or corporations, but the total of its direct loans and guarantees may not exceed its aggregate subscribed capital, surplus, and reserves.[1] It is obvious that the primary and major function of the bank is not to engage in direct loans, but to guarantee loans made by private individuals and institutions.

The aggregate volume of international loans and investments during the postwar period would almost certainly be greatly increased by the existence of the bank. The loans insured by it should offer a considerable degree of security to investors. Consequently, even after the payment of moderate commissions charged by the bank for guaranteeing loans,[2] funds should be available at a very reasonable interest rate.

Regulations covering the methods by which loans and guarantees may be extended appear to give significant assurance both that the principal and interest will be paid when due and that the funds will actually be employed for productive economic purposes.

Except in special circumstances, loans and guarantees cannot be made except for specific projects of reconstruction and development.[3] When a loan is made other than to the government of a member country itself, such a loan made or guaranteed by the bank must also be guaranteed as to the

---

[1] Article III, Sec. 3. This limit to the lending and guaranteeing power of the bank seems a most salutary proviso against uncontrolled pyramiding of the total of loans guaranteed by the bank, and hence against the danger that the bank's resources would be employed in an inflationary manner.

[2] The commission fee will be not less than 1 per cent nor more than 1.5 per cent during the first ten years [Art. IV, Sec. 5 (a)].

[3] The Research Committee of the CED, in a statement issued April 17, 1945, has recommended an extension of the bank's lending powers to serve the requirements of long-term monetary stabilization. On this point, the statement reads:

"We believe that the lending objective can be accomplished satisfactorily through the proposed International Bank for Reconstruction and Development,

repayment of principal and interest by the member concerned, by its central bank, or by a similar agency fully acceptable to the bank. This provision offers assurance that service of the bank's loan will have a high priority on the foreign-exchange resources of the borrowing country. In effect, this might require exchange control, import quotas, appropriate domestic fiscal policies, or a combination of all three to reduce imports of luxuries and nonessentials to the advantage of imports of capital equipment. It represents a very useful device for enabling relatively undeveloped countries to pay from their own resources for imported real capital.

Another important safeguard against wasteful employment of the bank's resources is that funds borrowed from the bank must be left on deposit at the bank and will be paid out only to meet the expenses of the project or undertaking for which the funds are lent. Every effort is made to impress borrowers with the fact that loans are to be repaid.

---

although we do recommend some extension of its powers. The purposes of the bank as stated do not seem to be sufficiently broad to include loans expressly intended to serve the requirements of long-continuing stabilization. We feel that the purposes should be so broadened.

"The needed general stabilization loans which would assist in orderly monetary relations might be of two sorts. There will probably be a need for long-term loans of a type for which there will be no provision at present under either the bank or the monetary fund. The bank's loans, as at present provided, are to be for specific projects of reconstruction or development; but there will probably be a number of countries that will need some more general form of loan assistance than these specific projects imply—loans designed to provide for imports of a variety of goods and services *in a general restoration of a country's powers of production and trade.* There may also be a need for short-term credits to assist in the maintenance of orderly relations in currency transactions themselves. These short-term credits may be particularly needed toward the end of the transition period, as nations proceed to relax their exchange controls and to find the equilibrium rates of exchange to which their international accounts could be balanced in a freer exchange market.

"The managers of the fund require and deserve the protection to the clarity of their operation that would come from clear authority to the bank to make loans for stabilization purposes when they are justified.

"Otherwise, there will be pressure on the managers of the fund to permit transactions not consistent with the short-term stabilization operations of a currency fund."

The bank may make direct loans to, or guarantee loans made to, any member government or political subdivision thereof, and to any business, industrial, or agricultural enterprise in the territory of a member nation. It must be satisfied, however, that the borrower would not otherwise be able to obtain the loan at a reasonable rate of interest. Before a loan can be extended or guaranteed, a competent committee must submit a written report recommending the project after a careful study of its merits.

It seems altogether likely that the bank will be in a much better position to judge the economic merits of a project for which a loan is requested than would a private investment bank or an investment syndicate. The cutthroat and uneconomical competition that sometimes characterized the placing of international loans, and which substantially added to the risk element, should happily be absent where loans are being requested from the bank.

The insurance feature of the lending operations of the bank is also important. Any loss that might be incurred through loans made or guaranteed by the bank would not fall upon individual investors or groups of investors or any one country. Instead, the loss would be spread over the countries in proportion to their capital participation in the bank.

The chance that a loan made or guaranteed by the bank might be repudiated by a borrower as the result of a general willingness to "despoil the foreigner" would be greatly lessened, since the bank will be the creature of a concert of nations, and repudiation would risk general international opprobrium. This is particularly important to the United States because the "Uncle Shylock" stigma was often applied to our attempts to obtain repayments of foreign loans during the period between the two world wars.

Loans to countries where the risk element is strong probably will be made almost exclusively through use of the bank's guarantee. This is not likely to be true, however, of good credit risks in the major countries where a large proportion of the loans will continue to be made without guarantee by the bank. It is also probable that in the case of bank guarantee of loans involving a higher risk element, the interest rate (including the bank's service commission) will be much smaller than the rate required if the funds were obtained from private sources. Paradoxically enough, the lower rate of interest should abate the vicious circle of high interest because of high risk, and high risk because of difficulty in paying high interest.

In general, loans provided by the bank will not be "tied loans."[1] That is, countries or the nationals of countries obtaining loans will be allowed to purchase the goods and services needed for the designated project in the markets of any country.[2] There is little doubt, however, that the value of goods and services purchased in the United States will tend to be at least as large as our capital subscription in the bank, because of the inevitably strong foreign demand for the types of goods we produce so efficiently.

Like the International Monetary Fund, the bank is one of the most important among the new international institutions that must be relied upon to further the expansion and stabilization of postwar international trade. The above analysis offers strong reasons for the United States government to ratify the agreement setting up the International Bank for Reconstruction and Development.[3]

---

[1] But the right of the member countries to deny permission for loans to be floated in their domestic money markets or to be made in terms of their particular currencies might possibly be used as a means of requiring that the proceeds of the loan be spent in the country in which the funds were raised.

[2] In any country except that of the borrower.

[3] Reference is again made to the qualifying footnote at the end of Chap. II.

The Research Committee of the Committee for Economic Development in its policy statement with reference to the Bretton Woods proposals has stated "We recommend the approval of the International Bank for Reconstruction and Development and also recommend that at an appropriate time, which would not delay its approval, its powers be broadened to include the extension of general long-term or short-term loans for stabilization purposes.

"After the Bank is strengthened in this way, we feel that the management of the Fund should be able to use the Fund strictly for currency transactions. Accordingly, the dangers inherent in the Fund as it now stands would be substantially reduced and we would recommend that the Fund be approved."

It is possible that the purpose of the recommendation in the policy statement of the Committee for Economic Development could be carried out without the necessity for formal reconsideration by the signatory countries. Existing phraseology would permit such loans under some circumstances.

The advantages of the proposal are considerable in removing pressure for loans from the Fund. The transfer of requests for advances from the Fund to the Bank would mean that the purposes for which advances were required could be examined somewhat more in accordance with conventional banking procedure.

It should be noted, however, that one of the admirable characteristics of the Bank is the way in which the resources of the Bank have been, as a general principle, reserved for use in connection with definite physical projects of an investment nature. It seems desirable that part of the resources of the Bank should be made available for loans for general stabilization purposes but that the amount of such loans should be restricted to some definitely limited part of the Bank's resources.

IV. THE NEWER FORMS OF TRADE
BARRIERS; THE GROWING
IMPORTANCE OF CARTELS
IN INTERNATIONAL TRADE

BETWEEN the two world wars, national intervention in
international trade assumed a quite different character
from that existing before 1914. For nearly a century, any
interference with "natural" currents of international trade
had been almost entirely in the form of protective tariffs and,
in some instances, subsidies to domestic producers. These
tariffs and subsidies reflected in some degree a survival of the
nationalism of the Mercantilists. To a larger extent, however,
they were simply the result of the scramble for special advantages or for survival on the part of each protected industry.
The type of national control of foreign trade that began to
develop following World War I was of a very different sort in
many ways; it represented a basic return to economic nationalism rather than a continuance of special protection to
individual industries.[1]

This great change in the character of national foreign trade
control was not simply a matter of resurrecting old control
devices or of developing new ones, such as exchange control,[2]
bilateral trade agreements, import quotas, special clearings
agreements, export subsidies, currency devaluations, and

[1] For a comprehensive description and critical analysis of these types of
foreign trade control see Jacob Viner, *Trade Relations between Free-market and
Controlled Economies*, League of Nations, Economic, Financial, and Transit
Department, Geneva, 1943.

[2] Exchange control usually involves the government's appropriation of the
foreign exchange which a national of the country obtains from the sale of goods
or services abroad, and his repayment for the appropriated exchange in the
national currency at a "pegged" rate. Importers must apply to the govern-

intergovernmental commodity agreements. These devices were resurrected, invented, or perfected as instruments for controlling foreign trade, but, almost invariably, the primary force behind them was the determination of the originating country to control its internal economy. The underlying objective might be self-sufficiency or industrialization, protection of the national balance of payments or, most important, elimination of unemployment.

The first notable and enormously important example of the new trend was set by Soviet Russia. Here was a complete departure—brought about by the most far-reaching and fundamental political and economic revolution in human history—from trade carried on by private individuals and corporations with only the minor intervention of governmental tariffs and subsidies. The Soviet state took over all industry and organized it into a series of trusts; and foreign trade was thenceforth operated as a state monopoly. Here was complete cartelization by the state. The state decided what imports were needed and then directed the exports necessary to pay for these imports. Capital construction was undertaken on an unprecedented scale, new industries were developed, and old industries expanded, with the purpose of making the Soviet Union economically independent. This program and policy continued to the present war and apparently is to be resumed after the close of hostilities.

Russian national self-sufficiency is not dependent upon tariff

---

ment for foreign exchange with which to make purchases abroad. Permission for such purchases is usually rigidly regulated. Exchange control is rarely a simple device, and as a rule includes some combination of exchange rationing, multiple exchange values as between any two currencies, export subsidies to offset the restrictive effect of overvaluation of currency on exports, clearing agreements, outright barter transactions, government operations on its own account outside the control, and other devices (*Ibid.*, p. 34). Indeed, "exchange control" has come to imply the whole complex of methods and mechanisms by which governments exercise direct and intimate control of foreign trade. In this study, the expression "exchange control and associated measures" usually is employed to express this concept.

protection of important industries. There could be no competition from foreign industries, either while new domestic industries were developing or afterwards, since the state did all buying and selling in foreign trade. There is little question that the success of the Soviet economic program depended upon this state monopoly of foreign trade, as a necessary complement to complete state control of domestic industry. In a very real sense it represented the absolute form of foreign trade control, attempted elsewhere in lesser degrees and on a smaller scale through tariffs, cartels, exchange controls, bilateral trade agreements, import quotas, multiple currencies, and special purchase agreements. In the case of National Socialist Germany, very much the same goals were achieved by these more complicated means.

A country operating its foreign trade as a state monopoly obviously can exploit its monopoly position both as buyer and as seller to extract the maximum advantage in barter terms of trade.[1] It has a great advantage in negotiating trade agreements with other governments, or in carrying out ordinary buying and selling transactions with individuals or corporations abroad. Like commercial monopoly, a state monopoly is in a favorable bargaining position when dealing with unorganized buyers and can organize its sales to maximize its returns. In its buyer role, the state monopoly can obtain its purchases at lowest cost in terms of the exports which it must offer in exchange. It may act as a "discriminating monopolist" in its purchases and sales—selling at different prices in different markets so as to maximize its receipts and buying at different prices in different markets to obtain its total supplies at minimum cost.

Using as a bargaining weapon its power to buy or not to buy the commodities of another country, a state monopoly

---

[1] A country that obtains an advantage in barter terms of trade is able thereby to procure a larger quantity of goods and services from another country for a given quantity of its own goods and services than if the advantage had not been secured.

can obtain preferential advantages for the sale of its own goods in the domestic market of that country. It may compel a country to remove a tariff or other trade barrier against its goods while the barriers are maintained against a competitor. The state monopoly is perfectly situated to carry out direct purchase agreements with particular countries, enhanced by highly discriminatory concessions. Further, a state trading monopoly lends itself easily to use as a weapon for extorting political or even military advantages. The principal use that Soviet Russia has made of the state trading monopoly has been, in fact, simply that of obtaining the best barter terms of trade, and its complete state control has been used in a much less militant and offensive[1] manner than the seemingly less absolute control in Germany, where exchange devices and associated measures were employed.

Some of the advantages in barter terms of trade that are obtainable by state monopoly and by exchange control can be obtained also by means of tariffs and tariff bargaining. Theoretically, by such bargaining methods a country could maximize the amount of goods and services it would be able to get in exchange for the goods and services it furnished. In practice, tariff bargaining and retaliation are usually more rigid and clumsy than bargaining through cartels or through exchange control and associated measures. The nation with a state monopoly of trade automatically and naturally takes advantage of the power of its single veto or assent, and individuals or corporations of other countries are perforce at a disadvantage in dealing with such a country.

The disadvantages which individuals or corporations have in dealing with a state monopoly of foreign trade are not wholly different from those attending trade with countries having tariffs, cartels, exchange control, bilateral agreements, or even private or corporate monopolies. These latter, in more or less complete degree, accomplish by more complicated methods the same purposes as the state monopoly of foreign

[1] In both meanings of the term.

trade, although the private or corporate monopoly may not be carried on for national advantage.[1]

The current style of intervention in, and control of, foreign trade on a large scale, but by less absolute means than those of a state monopoly of foreign trade, dates from the depression of the 1930's and was carried furthest by Nazi Germany. The motives for the comprehensive and intricate system of exchange controls, cartel agreements, bilateral agreements, and associated measures set up during the period from 1933 to the outbreak of the present war, were primarily and basically the creating of new industries and expanding of old ones in preparation for the war planned from the earliest moment of Nazi power. The system was also a scheme to eliminate unemployment.

The Nazis achieved a considerable and even impressive degree of success in arriving at the ends for which they inaugurated their complicated scheme of control of foreign trade. They furnished an important demonstration of the fact that it is very difficult—except for a country whose economic position is strong indeed—to maintain trading relations with a country that adopts such an armory of weapons for economic warfare as those employed by Germany except by employing similar weapons. Even so, countries in a poor strategic position economically are likely to be worsted in the conflict and compelled to accept the dictates of the economically stronger country.

A policy of selected imports was also made possible by the complicated system of foreign trade control associated with exchange control, which became almost universal immedi-

---

[1] In trading with a collective state such as Soviet Russia there is an advantage to the rest of the world that usually does not exist in the case of private or semi-private cartels. Goods are never pushed on the foreign market simply "in order to be got rid of." The volume of its exports is closely related to its desired volume of imports. Thus, if a collective state does attempt to obtain the best barter terms of trade, it does not attempt to sell as much as it can and buy as little as possible. (For noncollectivized countries the latter is often a greater nuisance than the former.)

ately before the present war. A variety of devices were used in different countries to achieve what had been one of the outstanding accomplishments of the Soviet foreign trade monopoly. The Soviet government has sold on the foreign market whatever goods it could spare internally, in order to obtain the foreign exchange to pay for tractors, machine tools, and raw materials—the selected imports necessary to carry forward the successive Five Year Plans. In the early 1930's, candy, eggs, furs, and other consumption goods were sold on the foreign market, though they would have been purchased eagerly by Soviet citizens had they been offered for sale on the domestic market. Petroleum products, lumber, and wheat were sold on world markets, notwithstanding the fact that they could have been used to great advantage domestically. Very little of the precious foreign exchange obtained in this way was used for the importation of consumption goods, though Soviet citizens would have been willing to pay fantastically high ruble prices for them.

Nazi Germany accomplished the same purpose through more devious methods. She was able to induce the Balkan governments to accept certain goods when often their citizens would have preferred others, while German purchases were limited largely to necessities like grain or to commodities of strategic military importance. But from France, whose economic position was not so weak, the Nazis were compelled to accept commodities like French champagne for a portion of the foreign exchange received from their sales there. By means of the new forms of foreign trade control, Germany was able to obtain the raw materials for an industrial boom while building up huge stock piles for war purposes as well.

THE CARTEL PROBLEM

Beyond state trading monopolies and comprehensive systems of exchange control, private and corporate monopolies, which normally take the form of the cartel, are significant in national economies and in the world economy.

Although no sharp line of division separates them, there are, of course, important differences between state trading monopolies, commodity agreements, and cartel arrangements with state participation and policing on the one hand and purely private cartels on the other. Participation by the state implies control in the public interest. The well-known evils of domestic cartelization are indeed intensified ordinarily if there is no control by the state. Higher prices to consumers, larger profits, lower total national wage income, idle capacity, limitations on new investment, and technical backwardness are likely to be the product of unregulated private monopoly. State control may mitigate these evils.

It is not an invariable rule, however, that state participation in cartel arrangements ensures control in the public interest. State participation might serve only to strengthen private monopoly if the control of the state is substantially in the hands of monopolists. Moreover, in the absence of international agreements, "the public interest" is almost certain to be the assumed public interest of the particular nation sponsoring the cartel. But the public interest of one country may be at variance with the public interest of other countries.

There can be little doubt that domestic cartelization and international cartelization are intimately interrelated. Private international cartels may diminish competition on the internal market and strengthen the economic forces favorable to domestic cartelization. Domestic cartelization may not directly produce international cartelization, but it does mean that any competition for international markets that may continue will be quite different in character from competition for international markets between individual corporations. It is one thing if scores of American, British, French, and German corporations producing steel, for instance, are all competing with each other for the market. It is quite another matter if the cartelized British steel industry competes as a unit in international trade with the cartelized steel industries of other countries. Even if—as seems unlikely—unrestrained competition between such giants continued to exist, it would not mean competition in the historic meaning of the word as used by economists.[1]

As is the case with governmental trading monopolies and systems of exchange control, it is possible through cartels to accomplish some of the things that can be done through more old-fashioned governmental tariffs. Indeed, cartels permit maneuvers not possible through tariffs alone, since cartels may control the foreign as well as the domestic market. However, tariffs often aid the monopolist in carrying out programs for the control of particular markets.

One of the simplest ways in which monopolies interfere with international trade is through a cartel agreement under which foreign cartelized producers agree to keep out of the domestic market on condition that the domestic cartel keeps out of certain markets abroad. If the domestic cartel is strong enough, such an agreement could entirely take the place of a protective tariff. On the other hand, a domestic monopolist usually finds his bargaining position (vis-à-vis outside monopolies) strengthened by a protective tariff on his product.

Indeed, if the cartel is protected by a sufficiently high tariff and is not threatened by domestic competition, it may be able to make a private "treaty" by which, in return for a promise to stay out of, say, Europe, it receives exclusive territory elsewhere (say in South America) in addition to its domestic market. The cartel might have enough bargaining power to make such a deal even though its domestic market were not protected by a tariff, but such a tariff is almost invariably a great help.

Corwin D. Edwards, at that time Chairman of the Policy Board of the Antitrust Division of the Department of Justice,

---

[1] This was a point made by Professor Gunnar Myrdal, Swedish economist, following a three-cornered discussion of the question by American, British, and Swedish economists.

speaking before the American Economic Association, January 23, 1944, quoted Sir Alfred Mond of Imperial Chemical Industries as follows:

In negotiation, the man behind the tariff wall always has something with which to bargain, which the man in the free-trade country has not. Any man who has any practical experience of bargaining with Continental producers knows that the first thing they say is, "You cannot export to our country because we have a tariff. How much of your market are you going to give us?"

Just how much of world trade is controlled by cartels or seriously affected by them is uncertain and has aroused much controversy.

Quoting further from Dr. Edwards's statement:

A substantial part of world trade before the war was controlled by cartels. Since 1939, the United States Department of Justice has instituted proceedings against thirty-seven such arrangements, having to do with petroleum, chemicals (including synthetic rubber, plastics, dyestuffs, nitrates, and explosives), pharmaceutical products, photographic materials, electric light bulbs, fluorescent lighting equipment, magnesium, molybdenum, titanium, tungsten carbide, aircraft accessories and instruments, military optical instruments, flexible metal hose, and quebracho. A tentative list of international cartel agreements which were in effect in 1939, prepared recently in this department, contains 179 such agreements, of which 109 included American enterprises.[1]

A cartel's bargaining power is measurably affected by its character, that is, whether it is purely private-corporate in character, whether it is counterbalanced by the government of the country in which the monopoly operates, whether it is assisted by the government, or whether, as the final degree,

[1] The Department of Justice has filed antitrust suits against a number of these alleged cartels. One of the first of these major suits was filed against the Imperial Chemical Industries, Ltd., of London, Imperial Chemical Industries, Ltd. (New York), E. I. du Pont de Nemours & Company, Inc., and the Remington Arms Co., Inc., on January 6, 1944.

the monopoly form is required by the government and used as a means of furthering the national interest. The cartels of Nazi Germany illustrate the final stage, serving not merely private profit-making ends but mainly Nazi national policy, economic and military. An intermediate form is illustrated by British cartels. These are not prohibited by British law but have even been promoted and have had their agreements policed by the British government.

The development of a great number and variety of forms of business and industrial associations in Great Britain—ranging from huge concerns, such as the Imperial Chemical Industries, down to the much looser forms of trade associations—has progressed much further than is generally realized. It has been accelerated by the war, which has necessitated the concentration of the production of particular types of goods in selected plants, with comprehensive regulations covering management and the allocation of earnings among the participating companies. It has been furthered by the industrial and commercial groupings formed to facilitate governmental supervision and control of production and marketing. However, these wartime developments only continue a trend that was already very pronounced under the prewar Chamberlain government. The British would argue that this program is an attempt to attain some of the production and marketing efficiency achieved by our own great corporations.[1] It

---

[1] A struggle seems to be shaping up in Great Britain between the Labor Party, led on this issue by Herbert Morrison, and the British industrialists. It is interesting to observe that the issue is not really whether centralization and cartelization of industry shall continue. That is pretty much taken for granted by both sides, although there is difference of opinion upon their degree and extent. Morrison argues that centralization of industrial control would be unthinkable without a high degree of state control. Indeed, Morrison favors a virtual socialization of the large centralized industries. The industrialists themselves, however, insist upon a large measure of industrial self-rule. The extreme point of view was expressed by a leader of one of the most highly centralized industries who was reported to have said: "All we ask of the government is to furnish us the markets, through tariff protection and trade bargaining. We will take care of everything else ourselves."

certainly seems to reflect a shrinking from the rigors of competition and a search for security upon the part of British industry.

Many British industrialists are aware, on the other hand, that extreme forms of cartelization inevitably must produce a high degree of governmental control and seek, therefore, to avoid such extreme forms while accepting some degree of regulation. Should domestic cartelization continue to develop in Great Britain after the war, however, it is difficult to see how one policy could be followed internally and another internationally. Would individual firms cartelized for domestic purposes be required to dissociate and to operate independently in the foreign field?

At least one wing of British industry favors a highly cartelized international trade. The British government itself apparently has not yet made up its mind on the matter. There is considerable evidence that its final position will be greatly affected by its future political and economic relations with the United States. The British government is well aware of the public hostility to cartels and all monopoly forms in the United States, although that hostility has sometimes been impotent against actual industrial practices. It appears that if the British government has reasonable expectation of an international trade revival on the basis of international tariff reductions, international currency agreements, and banks for international investment, accompanied by national programs of full employment, it may reject the cartel device as a means for carrying on British foreign trade. If such a general program for furthering international trade fails to eventuate, the cartelization of British foreign trade, in all probability, will persist and increase.

AMERICAN CARTEL POLICY

However ineffectively the Sherman Antitrust Act and other antimonopoly legislation have been enforced in the United States, public opinion remains strongly, if diffusely, antitrust and anticartel. To a considerable degree, the opposition is related to the name "cartel." For example, the United States has participated in commodity agreements covering wheat and coffee. It might be argued that these agreements are fundamentally different from those entered into by the chemical industry of the United States with the chemical industry of Great Britain. The arguments might stress that the wheat and coffee commodity agreements seek to protect the interests of hundreds of thousands of individual producers, without distress to the interests of any like producer, instead of fencing in production and markets for a handful of large corporations. Nevertheless, some commodity agreements would be difficult to distinguish from cartels. Yet no such odium attaches to their name as to that of cartels.

Since 1933, various countries have entered into commodity agreements in wheat, tin, sugar, tea, coffee, beef, timber, and rubber. Usually these were agreements between the governments of exporting countries, intended to support, or raise, particular prices through control of production, allocation of production quotas, marketing practices, and so forth. Occasionally the producers themselves are parties to the agreements. At other times, as in the case of wheat, beef, and coffee agreements, a consuming country is a party of the "treaty."[1]

In some cases representatives of a whole industry will negotiate a "gentlemen's agreement" with the industry of another country, with the more or less tacit blessing of the two governments. Such an agreement was signed in January, 1937, by the Cotton Textile Institute, Inc., representing American manufacturers, and by representatives of the Japanese industry.[2] The Japanese textile industry under-

---

[1] See *Intergovernmental Commodity Control Agreements*, International Labour Office, Montreal, 1943.

[2] Other agreements covered hosiery, cotton, velveteens, and corduroys. An earlier agreement, signed in 1935, restricted imports of cotton piece goods into the Philippines. See the discussion of voluntary or informal quotas in Percy W. Bidwell, *The Invisible Tariff: a Study of the Control of Imports into the United States*,

took to limit its shipments of piece goods to 100 million square yards each year. It seems reasonable to suppose that there are other somewhat similar informal agreements that escape general public notice.

Under the Webb-Pomerene Act, American exporters are allowed to form associations and to carry on foreign trade activities otherwise forbidden by our antitrust laws on condition that they do not thereby restrain trade in our domestic market or the trade of independent American exporters.

Many American concerns have entered into agreements with foreign cartels, apparently in the belief that, so long as they did not restrain domestic trade or exclude other American exporters from the foreign market, they were not illegal. Exchange of patent rights, often attending such participation, has been notorious as a means of implementing the cartel agreement.

The Department of Justice has brought a number of actions against American corporations for violations of the antitrust law, which, it is charged, were not covered by the protection of the Webb-Pomerene Act. Considerable sentiment has even developed within the present administration for the repeal of the Webb-Pomerene Act and for a comprehensive and vigorous attack against cartels in foreign trade.

American firms engaged in foreign trade claim that their position is difficult if not intolerable under present conditions. They argue that a foreign country may require that a company doing business there join a cartel and observe its regulations that may have the force of law. On the other hand, transaction with cartels or with corporations belonging to cartels may make American firms liable to prosecution under American law.

It is difficult to judge the validity of these complaints. No one could reasonably argue that we should rigidly enforce

prepared under the auspices of The American Coordinating Committee for International Studies, Council on Foreign Relations, New York, 1939, pp. 134–140.

anticartel legislation against our own nationals while taking no action whatever against foreign cartels. Indeed, no one does so argue. The Department of Justice has taken action against foreign cartels as well as against American concerns accused of participation in cartel agreements. Nevertheless, it is highly questionable whether the jurisdiction of the Department of Justice over foreign cartels in respect to activities carried on outside the United States can be made effective.

At present, no sovereign remedy for the cartel problem seems feasible. Like so many other aspects of international trade, cartels can hardly remain either unregulated or subject only to national control and regulation. An international conference to clarify the various national policies toward cartels and to take initial steps toward solution of the problem would be desirable. Such a conference might recommend the elimination of most cartels by national governments on the basis of international agreement. It could advise whether particular commodity agreements deserved international toleration or even support. It might suggest that certain activities usually carried on by cartels or under commodity agreements be permitted within limits and under national or international regulation.

On the basis of the deliberations of a preliminary international conference on cartels, a permanent commission for continued study and regulation might be established. As a minimum, such a commission might require that cartel-type agreements among corporations carrying on international trade be registered with the commission. The information thus obtained could provide the basis for more comprehensive regulation by member governments or by the commission itself. Until such time, the United States government might well require the registration of all agreements under which our nationals participate in international cartels.

The cartel problem is at an uncomfortable and even acute stage from the standpoint of American corporations engaged in foreign trade. The setting up of an international commission to deal with the problem is, consequently, particularly urgent.

From the long-run viewpoint the effect of cartels upon barter terms of trade is important, particularly for countries confronted with difficulties in financing imports vital to their domestic economies. Fortunately, this is not a pressing problem for the United States. Our tendency toward an unwieldy export surplus presents its own problems; but it does at least reduce the necessity for national concern about our aggregate barter terms of trade.

It has been pointed out frequently that the growth of cartels, like the growth of other recent forms of interference with and control of foreign trade, has been stimulated by the existence of overcapacity and unemployment.[1] Success in carrying out national programs of full employment might be expected to diminish materially the urge to form cartels, and to facilitate greatly the development of both a national and an international cartel policy. International agreement setting up institutions to facilitate international trade, such as the International Monetary Fund and the International Bank for Reconstruction and Development, would discourage further the tendency toward cartelization of international trade. Finally, agreement on the reduction and amelioration of tariffs, exchange controls, and associated measures would also contribute toward the same end. It may be necessary for the United States to use its bargaining power in these related matters to induce foreign governments to modify their national policy toward cartels.

[1] See the very useful article by Dr. Edward S. Mason, "The Future of International Cartels," *Foreign Affairs*, July, 1944, pp. 604–615. Dr. Mason is now engaged in a comprehensive study of the cartel problem for the Committee for Economic Development.

V. OUR TARIFF POLICY

REDUCING our protective tariff is an essential to any effective international program for expanding world trade. Protective duties are the principal form of trade control in which we have indulged.[1] We have made relatively little peacetime use of exchange control, import quotas, bilateral agreements, clearing agreements, and the like. This moderation is not attributable to superior international morality but is due to the fact that we relied upon domestic measures primarily in dealing with the unemployment of the depression. It could not have been claimed reasonably that our recovery program would have been seriously jeopardized by the imports of manufactured goods that could scale our high tariff walls.[2] Furthermore, our balance-of-payments position was such that we had little cause for concern about our supplies of essential imports. No special measures were necessary to ensure these supplies.[3]

Unemployment combined with balance-of-payments difficulties accounts largely for the new and comprehensive con-

[1] There are a good many exceptions, however. We have used sanitary regulations as a device for excluding foreign-produced commodities. We did devalue our currency in 1933 in an effort to stimulate exports. We have resorted to subsidies for the export of agricultural commodities. We have laws requiring preference for domestically produced goods in government purchases. We have import quotas on some commodities.

[2] Still, it must be admitted that we were not willing to take any risks in the matter. Both the National Industrial Recovery Act and the Agricultural Adjustment Act provided against increased imports that might hamper measures aimed at raising the price of American-produced goods.

[3] Even though we limited ourselves to simpler forms of trade barriers than those used by most other countries, we played a prominent role in the movement toward more varied and higher trade barriers. It would be too simple to credit the Smoot-Hawley tariff of 1930 with the major responsibility for the subsequent upsurge in trade restrictions, yet the enactment of this tariff did accelerate the movement toward trade restrictions.

trols of foreign trade which, by the outbreak of the present war, had become all but universal. Countries were confronted by a choice between enlarged unemployment and possible inability to pay for essential imports, on the one hand, and a departure from unrestricted foreign trade practices on the other. Eventually, and almost without exception, they chose the latter.

The recollection of how these newer forms of trade control came into existence may shed light on how they may be removed. These controls can be supplanted only by measures that will guarantee wide and stable employment and a reasonable balance in international payments. There can be no doubt about the choice almost all countries would make if they felt that the surrender of the comprehensive control of their foreign trade would cause a recurrence of widespread unemployment and an acute scarcity of foreign exchange.

Fortunately, an international program is taking shape which inspires hope that nations will not be faced with this choice. The main features of this program were outlined in the summary prefacing this study. They include establishment of the International Monetary Fund for the stabilization of exchange rates and for orderly adjustment of initial provisional rates. Eventual abolition of exchange controls is contemplated but conditions are specified under which, should the need arise, they may be partially restored. The International Bank for Reconstruction and Development is recommended as a means for easing the balance-of-payments problem. Preliminary study is directed to the problem of cartels; it seems probable that an international commission for further investigation and ultimately for regulation of cartels will be instituted. Finally, there is almost universal agreement that each nation must plan and put into execution measures to maintain full employment, of which the action of the United States would be by far the most important.[1]

[1] Although full employment is the most important factor in the revival of

Consequently, the lowering of our protective tariff should not be considered as a project independent of other international measures for expanding trade. It is an indispensable element of the larger program (outlined above) and a critical factor in its success. The markets of the United States are vital to a world desiring multilateral trade. No other national currency was so universally in demand or relatively so scarce in international trade as were dollars during the prewar years. This reflected both the desire of almost all peoples to purchase American commodities and the superiority of the dollar as a means of payment in almost all markets.

Countries like Great Britain, the Netherlands, Belgium, Norway, and Sweden have no means other than international trade for obtaining the raw materials, foodstuffs, and capital equipment needed for a tolerable national livelihood. The so-called "one commodity" countries, like Brazil, the Argentine, Chile, Malaya, and the Dutch East Indies, obtained both essential consumer goods and capital equipment through international trade. The possibility of improving the living standards of these countries is closely tied to the success of an international program for trade expansion. Because of the enormous importance of our domestic market, the lowering of our tariff constitutes a key factor in such a program.

We have repeatedly assured other countries of our intention to participate in concerted action for raising national standards of living through the removal of trade barriers. In proclaiming the Atlantic Charter, President Roosevelt and the British Prime Minister committed the two countries to the following (the fourth, fifth, and sixth articles of the charter):

Fourth, they will endeavor, with due respect for their existing obligations, to further the enjoyment by all states, great or small, victor or vanquished, of access, on equal terms, to the trade and to

---

international trade, measures by which it might be attained in the United States are largely of a domestic nature and are not likely to require control of our foreign trade. Therefore, an analysis of this problem is outside the scope of this study.

the raw materials of the world which are needed for their economic prosperity.

Fifth, they desire to bring about the fullest collaboration by all nations in the economic field with the object of securing, for all, improved labor standards, economic adjustment, and social security.

Sixth, after the final destruction of the Nazi tyranny, they hope to see established a peace which will afford to all nations the means of dwelling in safety within their own boundaries, and which will afford assurance that all men in all the lands may live out their lives in freedom from fear and want.

"Access, on equal terms, to the trade and to the raw materials of the world . . . " is both indefinite and broad. As far as the United States is concerned, it has been interpreted abroad to mean a reduction of tariffs and the granting of loans to permit the purchase of raw materials and capital goods.

Further declarations by President Roosevelt with respect to the four freedoms, including freedom from want, have been similarly interpreted. So have the statements by Vice President Wallace concerning our moral responsibility for improving living standards throughout the world. The declaration of the United Nations Conference on Food and Agriculture, in which official representatives of this government participated, included this statement:

The first cause of hunger and malnutrition is poverty. It is useless to produce more food unless men and nations provide the markets to absorb it. There must be an expansion of the whole world economy to provide the purchasing power sufficient to maintain an adequate diet for all. With full employment in all countries, enlarged industrial production, the absence of exploitation, and increasing flow of trade within and between countries, an orderly management of domestic and international investment and currencies, and sustained internal and international economic equilibrium, the food which is produced can be made available to all people.[1]

[1] United Nations Conference on Food and Agriculture, Hot Springs, Va.,

The long campaign led by Secretary Hull for the removal of tariff barriers has added its weight to world expectation that the United States will lead in facilitating and expanding the international exchange of goods and services.

Above all, lend-lease has strengthened the hope, already voiced in many parts of the world, that the United States will assume the primary responsibility for providing in some way the means by which all countries can pay for the goods and services that they want to import from us. This might be done by opening up a market here for their goods and increasing our imports, or it might be accomplished by loans. At all events, the belief that the United States has promised to do this in one way or another is widespread. This opinion is confirmed by the specific references in the lend-lease agreements to contemplated improvement of international trade.

Our frequent references to the need to assist other countries in raising their living standards may well have aroused erroneous expectations. Stable and dependable international economic relations cannot be founded upon charity. In the long run, only an economic policy that serves enlightened national interest[1] will receive support from our own people or respect from other nations.

Our tariff reduction is important to other countries, but would it be in our own national economic interest? As part of a general international program for expanding world trade, it would indeed be in our national interest. We might reasonably expect an appreciable increase in our national income as a result.[2] The first objection to such a course will be that it might cause unemployment in the United States.

May 18 to June 3, 1943, *Final Act and Section Reports*, U.S. Government Printing Office, Washington, D.C., 1943, p. 11.

[1] The national interest *from the long-term point of view*.

[2] No Utopian expectations should be entertained, however, of great reductions in our cost of living or of dramatic increases in our national income as a direct result of lowering our tariff by the percentages likely in the immediate future. During the last few decades our experience with tariff changes, either through the passage of new tariff acts or through the negotiation of trade agreements,

There is no denying that, if the lowering of our tariffs were effective, it would result in some unemployment in industries depending on tariffs for sales prices high enough to cover costs.[1] Actually, however, this unemployment would be offset by increased employment in industries producing for export. This may be expected because foreign nationals would have increased purchasing power from expanded sales in this country. Experience of the past decades indicated that the volume of foreign purchases in the United States is dictated very largely by the amount of dollar exchange available abroad. Increased purchases by foreigners are made more likely by the fact that our tariff reduction would (and should) involve reciprocal though not necessarily proportionate reductions in the tariffs and other trade barriers of other nations.[2]

---

does not indicate large changes in the volume of imports attributable directly to variations in tariff rates on particular commodities.

Tariff reduction by the United States becomes a matter of significance when viewed as part of a general movement toward the expansion of world trade synchronized with high levels of domestic employment in the various countries of the world.

[1] In many cases industries have a quite unnecessary "protection," since their costs are actually below those of foreign producers. The removal of this protection would matter little except where it was being used to protect a domestic monopoly. Even an industry dependent on tariff protection would not, in most instances, go out of production completely were the protection removed. The most inefficient, high-cost enterprises might be forced out of production first, while other lower cost, more efficient units might still compete without tariff protection. Our experience during the depression offered some evidence, however, that the marginal producer is not always forced out first. By wage cuts and other desperate means these marginal producers often hung on as long as the more efficient enterprises.

[2] Lowering of our tariffs should be made contingent upon similar action by other countries. Our insistence upon reciprocal action would be not only in our own national interest but in the general international interest as well. Our present bargaining power can be extremely useful in obtaining a general reduction of tariffs, exchange controls, and of all forms of restrictions on foreign trade. The tendency toward a surplus in our balance of payments precludes the necessity for hard bargaining.

It may be necessary to make allowance for protective tariffs or domestic subsidies in industrially backward countries, such as China, India, and the

There can be no denial of the social cost involved in the transfer of men, management, and capital from one industry to another, even if total employment is not reduced. In consequence, advocates of tariff removal or reduction often are eloquent enough in support of freedom of international trade in general but turn coy when it comes to the question of citing specific industries in which employment may be reduced. No one likes to advocate reduction in employment in the raw wool, sugar, copper, textile, or clothing industries, for example, even though the expansion of employment in the production of automobiles, electrical goods, steel, and aluminum would be sufficient to offset such unemployment and the compensating employment would be at a higher wage level.

A strong argument can be made for providing governmental compensation where lowering of the existing protective tariff causes the market of a particular industry to disappear. Such compensation might likewise be needed for unemployed labor and for obvious losses incurred by family-sized farms and ranches in shifting production.

Our fear of tariff reduction arises chiefly from the fact that general unemployment has been so frequent and on such a scale that persons displaced through curtailment of production in one industry could not feel confident of employment in another. Domestic economic policies that would succeed in preventing depression-type unemployment would greatly lessen this fear psychosis. Some years of experience with favorable employment conditions might consequently permit the lowering of trade barriers on a scale now precluded by our inhibitions.

In the immediate postwar period acceptance of lowered protective tariffs should be facilitated by the realization that additional imports induced by such action would be small in

Latin American countries, in order to stimulate the growth of new industries. This should be permitted only where these industries give promise of attaining an authentic comparative advantage when once firmly established.

volume for one year or two at least. This period of grace would tend to ease the transition from high tariff protection to lower tariffs.

Because of the possible social cost involved in the transfer of men, management, and capital from one employment to another, negotiations for the removal or lowering of international trade barriers should try to avoid large and sudden dislocations or to assure that transfers shall be as gradual as is consistent with substantial progress. This reasoning leads inevitably to the question of the method by which a reduction in our protective tariff might be achieved.

BILATERAL TRADE AGREEMENTS *vs.* MULTILATERAL AGREEMENTS FOR TARIFF REDUCTION

Bilateral trade agreements, as they have been negotiated in the past, have been agreements between pairs of countries, providing for varying degrees of tariff reduction on a product-by-product basis. Such bilateral agreements permit flexible and selective treatment of commodities and tariff reductions. This means that a country may choose to reduce the tariff on those commodities in which the total domestic production is small, in order to avoid the social costs of even temporary unemployment. Such procedure, of course, lessens the beneficial effects as well as the harmful effects of tariff reduction. Indeed, if tariff reductions were limited to this type of action, the shift in national resources toward more effective employment would not be sufficient to achieve any substantial increase in our national real income.

Nevertheless, the advantages of this method are not negligible. For example, if a trade agreement results in lowering our tariff on vegetables imported from some Caribbean country at a season when hardly any such vegetables are produced in this country, and in return the tariff on imports of our lard is lowered by that country, there may be an increase in the consumption of both lard and vegetables in each of the two countries, without significantly increasing competition for the vegetable farmers in the United States. This example may seem remote, but the same principle operates in many actual cases. Transitional unemployment may be mitigated if the trade barriers selected for reduction are those that protect only a few producers but operate to raise prices high enough to limit consumption severely. Moreover, when particular commodities form the subject of these special trade agreements between two countries, it is possible to forecast the specific results of the agreement. In multilateral reduction of tariffs, following some general formula, forecasting is difficult and precise estimates of beneficial and adverse effects are likely to prove unreliable.

Tariff reduction through a resumption of our reciprocal trade-agreements program after the war would be a conservative approach to the problem. The negotiation of such agreements is time-consuming. Furthermore, a country may not be ready to lower its tariff or other trade barriers except upon a multilateral basis. Thus, the extent to which Great Britain might be willing to lower trade barriers against automobiles imported from the United States might conceivably depend upon whether or not we were prepared to lower our tariff on vegetable oils produced by some colonial country which in turn imported British textiles.

The negotiation of triangular or even multiangular trade agreements embodying the principle of reciprocity would not be impossible. But to do it product by product, taking account of the various possible combinations, would require the maximum of patience and ingenuity in negotiation if indeed it would be feasible at all except perhaps as a part of a general international undertaking seeking to eliminate trade barriers.

The reciprocal trade-agreements program has the practical advantage that it already has had Congressional approval, and progress under its provisions could begin without raising a domestic political storm. Indeed, regardless of whether or not some more ambitious and more comprehensive program of a multilateral nature is attempted, the reduction of tariffs through the renewed negotiation of reciprocal trade agreements should be continued.

An international conference that would negotiate an agreement for the multilateral reduction of tariffs and for the elimination of exchange controls, import quotas, and other associated measures would be a move toward greater progress in freeing the channels of trade. It is well to remember, however, that it is hardly possible to induce other countries to abandon the quantitative control of their imports in addition to lowering their tariffs, without our offering substantial tariff cuts in return. A general formula that made multilateral reduction of trade barriers feasible can be expected to face opposition by many special-interest groups in the United States as well as in other countries.

The choice of a general formula for lowering tariffs presents serious technical difficulties. The simplest formula, at least in terms of statement, would be a uniform percentage reduction of all tariffs from their existing levels. This has the drawback of reducing both low tariffs and high tariffs in the same proportion. Thus, it would be unfair to low-tariff countries and to low-tariff industries. Another suggested formula is the reduction of all duties by a fixed per cent of their prevailing rates or by a fixed per cent *ad valorem*, whichever would result in a lower duty, but with no reduction of duties required below a fixed percentage *ad valorem*. This formula has the advantage of bearing more heavily on the higher duties and less heavily on the lower duties. Consequently, it would not have the effect of penalizing countries with already low tariffs. But it has a number of disadvantages, one being that it would tend to impair the existing tariff structure by disturbing the relation among the tariffs on different commodities. Numerous other formulas have been proposed. No formula would solve all problems, and a great many exceptions would have to be made or very complicated formulas would have to be developed for special problems.[1]

As has been pointed out previously, an agreement for tariff reduction alone is meaningless in the case of a country like Soviet Russia where the economy is completely collectivized. Russia does not depend upon tariffs to regulate her trade. State agencies buy and sell when, where, and as much as the policy of the state dictates. The same holds true of the type of controlled economy that existed in Germany, Italy, and Japan before the war. Even for countries where in peacetime the economic system is not state-controlled, exchange control, bilateral agreements, import quotas, special purchase agreements, etc., may be more important than tariffs. Consequently, any lowering of our trade barriers should not proceed under agreements wherein other countries pledge merely a corresponding lowering of tariffs. In addition, there should be specific agreements eliminating other forms of barriers or restricting their use to limited periods after the war or to emergencies under specified conditions.[2] In the case of Soviet Russia, there might have to be an agreement that the USSR would take certain total quantities of goods at stipulated prices.

The varying degrees of cartelization in the countries participating in agreements to lower trade barriers and controls could hardly be ignored, since cartel agreements between organized national industries can accomplish very much the same sort of control as is accomplished by tariffs. Indeed, it is possible to do some things through cartels that mere

[1] Professor Winfield Riefler has suggested the advisability of legislation providing for the elimination of tariff protection in the case of products that do not affect the livelihood of more than a limited number of workers, say 500 men. This would make possible an increase of imports not likely to reduce employment in the United States in any important industry.

[2] In its various trade agreements with other countries, the United States government has developed a series of provisions intended to protect itself against these direct forms of foreign trade control. See Jacob Viner, *Trade Relations between Free-market and Controlled Economies*, League of Nations, Economic, Financial, and Transit Department, Geneva, 1943.

tariffs could hardly accomplish at all. Unless there is concerted action aimed at the elimination or regulation of
cartels, the program for lowering trade barriers would be
substantially retarded.

Finally, the usefulness of agreements for lowering trade
barriers would be greatly circumscribed if each country were
free to alter the exchange value of its currency at will. Were
we free to lower the exchange value of the dollar in relation to
the pound, we might be able to nullify to a considerable degree
the effects of a reduction in our tariffs. Conversely, were the
British free to lower the exchange value of the pound sterling
in terms of the dollar, the results of any accepted tariff policy
on their part might be largely offset. Fortunately, the
International Monetary Fund plan points the way to a possible solution of this problem.[1]

The level of foreign-exchange rates also might affect the
volume of our imports and exports considerably. Thus, if a
pound-dollar rate were agreed upon which, at the existing
price levels in the United States and Great Britain, enabled
the British to sell goods cheaply in terms of dollars in the
United States and at the same time meant high prices in
terms of pounds for American goods sold in Great Britain,
our large net export surplus might be reduced somewhat even
if our tariff were not lowered. However, the subsequent
increase in sales of British goods in the United States might
be limited inasmuch as the demand for British goods in our
markets might be so nearly inelastic that the decreases in price
might not attract enough demand to compensate for the lower
dollar price per unit. Consequently, the total returns to the
British economy from a low pound-dollar ratio would be
uncertain.[2]

[1] Ratification of the agreement setting up the International Monetary Fund
would not solve this problem completely, but it would help considerably.
Countries may devalue their currencies but only under conditions of notification and according to procedure set up in the statutes of the fund.

[2] See also Hal B. Lary and Associates, *The United States in World Economy*,
Economic Series 23, United States Department of Commerce, Bureau of Foreign

Paradoxically, it is true that most countries, though they will gain even more than we from the expansion of international trade, will probably have to be persuaded both through inducements and through pressure to participate in a program of trade-barrier reduction. Many of these countries will be confronted with the problem of whether or not they will be able to carry out reconstruction, industrialization, or measures ensuring full employment without protection of trade barriers. They will be willing to lower trade barriers only if they are convinced that the world economic and political climate is favorable and only if they are assured that international economic arrangements will reduce the need for their national economic controls. If there is a promise of a peaceful world, if there are determined efforts on the part of all important countries to carry forward dynamic programs of full employment, if the International Monetary Fund is approved by the major countries, if the minimum of international loans required for bridging the immediate postwar period can be arranged, if there are no holdouts among the important countries in lowering trade barriers, then the prospects for freer international trade will be very bright.

Lowering our own trade barriers would help solve one of the most difficult problems anticipated in international trade. Almost certainly we shall have a large export surplus during

---

and Domestic Commerce, Washington, D.C., 1943, pp. 15, 175–176, 182. Important British exports to the United States are whisky, cotton goods, flax, linen and jute manufactures, woolen cloth and apparel, and leather goods. Goods imported from the United Kingdom have been quality goods depending for sale more on their prestige than on their price. The import of these goods, as long as they remain in the luxury class, is more likely to be affected by the degree of prosperity in the United States than by changes in duties or in the exchange value of the pound.

On the other hand, in some instances lowering of the price might prove critical in moving some commodities out of the luxury class into the class of goods having a mass market. Imported goods now impeded by our tariff, such as ceramics, pottery, and bicycles, might likewise be benefited. In this connection see the pamphlet by Paul Bareau, *The Dollar Problem*, American Chamber of Commerce, London.

the first few years after the war, which, in part at least, will have to be financed by credit advanced by the United States or by our nationals. A lowered tariff permitting larger imports would reduce the amount of credit required to finance a given volume of exports and would facilitate somewhat the later repayment of credits advanced.

Assuming international good will, our participation and leadership in a movement for the removal of trade barriers would be highly desirable. In view of the expectations that have been aroused, it is particularly advisable that the United States should not bear the responsibility for possible failure of the movement toward freer international trade.

The worst possible policy for us to follow would be the one we have been widely accused of pursuing in the past, i.e., refusing to cooperate in the necessary steps for facilitating freer world trade, closing our markets more tightly against imported commodities while using high-pressure methods to expand the sales of our goods and services in foreign markets. This policy would certainly reap an abundant harvest of international ill will.

The alternative to freer international trade is a stronger movement toward centralized national control of the economic life in all countries. This might not affect the United States so directly, since we might be able to carry on without fundamental changes in our economic organization. It might, however, force less self-sufficient nations into economic-political alignments whose relations to the United States would be problematical and even inimical, particularly if we were considered responsible for the failure of an international program to remove trade barriers.

For example, if our economic policy does not permit them to obtain raw materials and other essential commodities through unobstructed international trade, the countries of Western Europe might form closer ties with Soviet Russia than with the United States. The countries of Eastern Asia and the adjacent islands might be prompted to form an economic and political bloc of their own if satisfactory trade relations with the United States and the rest of the world were not attainable.

It is essential that there should be full legislative sanction and responsibility for any program of international economic cooperation upon which we embark. It would be useless and inadvisable to approach other nations with a proposal for a conference aimed at a comprehensive agreement for multilateral reduction of tariffs and other trade barriers without definite assurance that such an agreement would be ratified by Congress. But while plans for an international conference for the multilateral lowering of trade barriers should be speeded, the Reciprocal Trade Agreements Act should be renewed and strengthened as a supplementary means for achieving the goal of expansion of international trade.[1]

Once an attempt at general and multilateral tariff reductions is made, some way must be found to avoid Congressional debate over each separate item and tariff schedule. The reciprocal trade agreements provided a means by which this could be done. If anything more comprehensive and more fundamental is undertaken, Congress should be consulted as negotiations are planned and are in progress, and any final and general agreement should be referred to Congress for ratification. Unless some such procedure is adopted, it is only too likely that legislative suspicion and hostility will prevent successful participation in any comprehensive international economic program.

[1] Strengthening of the Reciprocal Trade Agreements Act of 1934 would be provided by enactment of a bill now before Congress. This bill would extend the act for three more years. An amendment would relate the 50 per cent limitation on reductions of American tariff rates to the rates of 1945 instead of the rates of 1934. This would permit reductions in some instances of as much as 75 per cent from those in effect in 1934.

VI. OUR LEND-LEASE POLICY

Our fundamental mistakes in handling the settlement of the inter-Allied debts of World War I were, first, our failure to reach an early and definite agreement for funding these debts; second, our failure, when a funding agreement was finally made, to set amounts acceptable to public opinion in the countries making payments; finally, and most important, our failure to fund these debts at levels consistent with the amount of goods and services we were willing to accept in payment. The debtor countries felt that they were asked to make payments that in effect we refused to receive.

In considering a solution of the lend-lease problem that would avoid such mistakes, it is useful to review the facts of lend-lease. Up to July 1, 1944, the cost of the program to the United States was $28,270 million, of which actual shipments or services rendered had amounted to $21,534,870,000.[1] The remainder represented largely goods and services in transit or awaiting shipment. Of the total, Great Britain had received $9,321,549,000; Russia, $5,931,944,000; the Mediterranean theater, $3,070,829,000; India and China, $1,402,426,000; Australia and New Zealand, $1,011,885,000; and Latin America, $171,970,000. Reverse lend-lease, or goods and services furnished by our Allies as an offset to lend-lease during this same period, amounted to around $3 billion. This reverse lend-lease has consisted of supplies, services of the British merchant marine, the cost of barracks and other military installations used by our troops abroad, and similar items.

From the beginning of the program on March 11, 1941, to the end of March, 1944, the United States sent more than

[1] By December 31, 1944, the cost of lend-lease had increased to more than $35 billion (*The New York Times*, February 21, 1945). The total may reach $40 billion or even $50 billion, depending upon the length of the war with Japan.

30,000 planes, some 25,000 tanks, and over 500,000 other military motor vehicles to the recipients of lend-lease.[1] A later report shows that 1,400 naval ships, 511 merchant ships of over 1,000 gross tons, and 1,284 merchant ships of less than 1,000 gross tons had been furnished under lend-lease.[2]

More than one-half of all lend-lease aid has consisted of planes, tanks, ships, bombs, ammunition, and other implements of war; about 34 per cent has been industrial materials, products, and food; the balance were services, including the shipping of supplies and ferrying of planes to the battle fronts, servicing Allied ships, repairing damaged ships, building factories in the United States, manufacturing lend-lease equipment, training pilots for the air forces of our Allies, etc.

SHOULD LEND-LEASE BE CONTINUED AFTER THE WAR?

The ultimate total of lend-lease contributions will depend not only on the duration of the war, but also on whether such aid is continued after hostilities cease. Everyone appears to agree that there will be need for continuation of the mutual-aid program in connection with hostilities in the Pacific theater of war. Lend-lease aid on some scale to Great Britain, for example, is necessary for the most effective prosecution of the war against Japan. How great should this lend-lease aid be, however? Should we continue to furnish the same amounts of goods and industrial materials to Great Britain as we furnished before Germany's defeat? Above all, should we continue lend-lease to countries that fought with us against Germany but do not participate in the war against Japan?

Should lend-lease, as has been suggested by some, be continued as a permanent institution for facilitating international

---

[1] Office of Emergency Management, Foreign Economic Administration, *Lend Lease Act, Fifteenth Report to Congress on Lend-lease Operations for Period Ended March 31, 1944*, U.S. Government Printing Office, Washington, D.C., 1944.

[2] Quarterly report to Congress on lend-lease, as of June 30, 1944, as reported in the *The New York Times*, August 24, 1944.

trade and investment on a new basis? It has been argued that lend-lease will be required in the postwar period to provide relief, to aid in the rebuilding of war-wrecked countries, for capital equipment and specialized services if the less industrialized nations are to go forward, and, also, to afford an outlet for an inevitably large American export surplus.

Discontinuance of lend-lease will reduce tremendously our immediate exports. Our total exports, excluding deliveries to our armed forces, reached an all-time record total of $14 billion in 1944. Of this amount, lend-lease accounted for about 80 per cent.[1] There will probably be strong demand from some quarters for perpetuation of lend-lease under some other name. It should be fully realized, however, that lend-lease has been essentially a procedure for providing goods and services to foreign governments without payment. Evidence and logic support our having provided these goods and services for the most effective conduct of the war. However, when the war ends these reasons for lend-lease will disappear. Giving goods away in peacetime would not be international trade. The interests of our own citizens, in terms of their needs for additional goods and services or in terms of tax relief, should be considered as an alternative to what would amount to deficit spending for foreign account.

Lend-lease was conceived for the purpose of waging war against our enemies. Edward R. Stettinius's report to Congress puts it as follows:

Lend-lease is not a loan of money. Nor has it ever been an act of charity. The lend-lease program of providing goods and services to nations resisting the Axis aggressors was undertaken for the defense of this country and has been carried out in the interests of the people of the United States. We have aided other peoples under lend-lease because their interests coincided with our interest.[2]

[1] *The New York Times*, February 1, 1945, reporting release of information by the United States Department of Commerce.

[2] Edward R. Stettinius, Jr., *Report to the 78th Congress on Lend-lease Operations, from Passage of Act, March 11, 1941, to December 31, 1942*, U.S. Government Printing Office, Washington, D.C., 1943, p. 8.

To employ lend-lease as a permanent part of our peacetime international trade, *i.e.*, for nonmilitary purposes, would be a perversion of its original aim.

The United States will inevitably play a major role after the war in providing relief to war-torn countries, in furnishing both funds and equipment for reconstruction and development, and in facilitating the stabilization of foreign-exchange rates. Aid of this sort, however, should not be given under lend-lease but through the medium of such agencies as the United Nations Relief and Rehabilitation Administration, the International Monetary Fund, and the International Bank for Reconstruction and Development. These matters should be decided on merit and should not be confused with the military purposes of lend-lease.

It may well be that after the termination of hostilities there will remain need for large-scale assistance to foreign governments, other than that provided for or contemplated through existing or proposed governmental agencies. There can be little doubt, for example, that it is in our national interest that the British should be able to function economically, politically, and militarily as one of the great powers. If loans or other forms of advances are essential to this purpose, our national interest would appear to be served by making them.[1]

A $2.5 billion "drawing account" for purchase in the United States during the next eighteen months of goods useful for

---

[1] It is essential that lend-lease aid to the United Kingdom be continued after Germany's defeat, and the British government early made representations to that end. The *NAM News* of August 6, 1944, reported that British officials informed American leaders that such aid would be required to stave off a serious postwar economic situation in England and was essential if Britain is to play the part expected of her in the Pacific war. The reported cost to the United States was placed at $2.5 billion annually. The argument was advanced that in the prewar period the United Kingdom normally imported about $4 billion worth of goods and services, paid for through the income yielded by British foreign investments ($800 million), by shipping services ($500 million), by exports ($2,500 million), and by miscellaneous services. The British are reported to have argued that for some time after the defeat of Germany they will need substantial lend-lease or similar aid to narrow the gap caused by the

postwar reconstruction was recently arranged with the French government. Cash payments are to be made for 20 per cent of such purchases, the remainder to be paid for over a period of thirty years with interest at 2⅜ per cent.[1]

It is reported that the Soviet government has requested a credit of some $6 billion or $7 billion for the purchase of goods in the United States for postwar reconstruction and development.

The case for financial advances by the United States in these and similar instances will stem from political and diplomatic requirements of the postwar period. To confuse loans or other advances of this sort with lend-lease might impair the diplomatic usefulness of such loans as well as jeopardize the chances of repayment. To confuse loans of this type with lend-lease might also render difficult public acceptance of the principle of cancellation of bona fide wartime lend-lease aid.

REPAYMENT OF LEND-LEASE AID

The Lend Lease Act seems purposely vague about repayment. Section 3 (*b*) states:

The terms and conditions upon which any such foreign government receives any aid authorized under subsection (*a*) shall be those

---

decline of their exports, the liquidation of their investments abroad, and the deterioration of their position as the world's foremost shipper. This might imply a need for lend-lease or a similar form of aid for an indefinite period after the defeat of Japan if the economic and strategic role of the British government is to be maintained.

[1] These goods are to consist of raw materials, such as cotton and metals, petroleum products, food, locomotives, railroad cars, industrial equipment, and the like, considered to be essential to the prosecution of the war but of peacetime use also. Under the agreement, production and delivery of these goods will not have to stop even though the war ends before they are finished. It is understood between the two governments, however, that the United States has the right to cancel or revoke procurement programs or contracts if it is in the national interest to do so.

Whether the French government could place orders within the categories and amounts agreed upon after hostilities in Europe cease is not entirely clear. Presumably, the assurance given Congress by Leo T. Crowley, head of the Foreign Economic Administration, that lend-lease would not be used for postwar rehabilitation and reconstruction purposes would prevent this.

which the President deems satisfactory, and the benefit to the United States may be payment or repayment in kind or property, or any other direct or indirect benefit which the President deems satisfactory: provided, however, that nothing in this paragraph shall be construed to authorize the President in any final settlement to assume or incur any obligations on the part of the United States with respect to postwar economic policy, postwar military policy, or any postwar policy involving international relations except in accordance with established constitutional procedure.[1]

The master agreement between the governments of the United States and the United Kingdom on principles applying to mutual aid in the prosecution of the war (consummated on February 23, 1942) is more specific on the question of repayments.[2] The preamble, after stressing the mutual benefits of lend-lease, states:

And whereas it is expedient that the final determination of the terms and conditions upon which the Government of the United Kingdom receives such aid and of the benefits to be received by the United States of America in return therefor should be deferred until the extent of the defense aid is known and until the progress of events makes clearer the final terms and conditions and benefits which will be in the mutual interests of the United States of America and the United Kingdom and will promote the establishment and maintenance of world peace. . . . [3]

Article V of the master agreement provides:

The Government of the United Kingdom will return to the United States of America at the end of the present emergency, as determined by the President, such defense articles transferred under this agree-

---

[1] *Lend Lease Act*, as amended May 17, 1944, Sec. 3(*b*). The text of this act may be found in the *Fifteenth Report to Congress on Lend-lease Operations*, pp. 62–65. The proviso at the end of this section is an amendment passed by overwhelming majority in Congress in the spring of 1944.

[2] Identical master lend-lease agreements have been signed with Belgium, China, Czechoslovakia, Ethiopia, Greece, Liberia, the Netherlands, Norway, Poland, Soviet Russia, and Yugoslavia. Australia and New Zealand have accepted the principles of these agreements.

[3] *Fifteenth Report to Congress on Lend-lease Operations*, p. 66.

ment as shall not have been destroyed, lost or consumed and as shall be determined by the President to be useful in the defense of the United States of America or of the Western Hemisphere or to be otherwise of use to the United States of America.[1]

Article VII of the master agreement, however, succeeds in entangling the settlement of lend-lease with most of the economic and political problems of the postwar world. It reads as follows:

In the final determination of the benefits to be provided to the United States of America by the Government of the United Kingdom in return for aid furnished under the Act of Congress of March 11, 1941, the terms and conditions thereof shall be such as not to burden commerce between the two countries, but to promote mutually advantageous economic relations between them and the betterment of world-wide economic relations. To that end, they shall include provision for agreed action by the United States of America and the United Kingdom, open to participation by all other countries of like mind, directed to the expansion, by appropriate international and domestic measures, of production, employment, and the exchange and consumption of goods, which are the material foundations of the liberty and welfare of all peoples; to the elimination of all forms of discriminatory treatment in international commerce, and to the reduction of tariffs and other trade barriers; and, in general, to the attainment of all the economic objectives set forth in the Joint Declaration made on August 12, 1941, by the President of the United States of America and the Prime Minister of the United Kingdom.[2]

The provisions of this master agreement indicate that in the final settlement of lend-lease the United States government wishes to avoid accentuating the heavy passive balance of foreign countries (especially the United Kingdom) vis à vis

---

[1] *Ibid.*, p. 67. Article VI declares that "in the final determination of the benefits to be provided to the United States of America by the Government of the United Kingdom full cognizance shall be taken of all property, services, information, facilities, or other benefits or considerations provided by the Government of the United Kingdom subsequent to March 11, 1941, and accepted or acknowledged by the President on behalf of the United States of America."

[2] *Ibid.*, p. 68.

the United States. Subsequent statements by our governmental leaders have been in similar vein and, incidentally,
have probably aroused expectations that may be somewhat
difficult to fulfill.

One thing is clear about the terms of lend-lease: we have
repeatedly given the debtor countries cause for believing that
we shall be very generous. In view of this, what principles
may guide us toward a reasonable settlement?

1. *We should require no repayment whatever for goods and services
that have been consumed up to the cessation of hostilities.* Public
opinion in the debtor countries certainly would not approve
repayment of this type of lend-lease aid. It is impossible,
obviously, to compare the costs of war in different nations.
There is no common denominator for money, goods, lives,
personal hardships, and the like. It seems reasonable that
we should write off the cost of goods already used up by our
active Allies.

Even if the governments and peoples of the countries that
have contracted huge debts under lend-lease were willing to
pay in full, the means of payment would not exist. We should
be unwilling certainly to accept, during any reasonably short
period, the tremendous volume of goods and services that
would be required to liquidate a major part of the indebtedness. Such disruption of international trade and of our
domestic economy is out of the question. Gold holdings of
the debtor countries are insufficient to clear the lend-lease
debt, apart from the fact that the greater portion of the
existing reserves could not be devoted to this end. Finally,
were it possible to be paid fully in gold, the gold would add
little to our real national wealth.

2. *It seems reasonable, however, for us to require either repayment
or return of lend-lease goods that are still in existence and that have
value either for peacetime purposes or as a part of national armaments.*

a. All lend-lease goods that would be of use to our own
forces in the war against Japan should be repossessed unless
they are employed by the recipient nation in the war against

Japan. An acceptable alternative would be the offer of reasonable payment for such goods by the recipient country.

b. All goods on order or in transit but not yet delivered should be retained by the United States, except when the prospective recipient nation accepts the principle that such goods are to be paid for eventually.

c. All other lend-lease goods should be disposed of for the best price obtainable. In most cases this would mean selling the goods to the country that had received them under lend-lease. However, if the net return from the sale of, say, a million blankets would be greater by selling blankets now in England to the Norwegian government or to Norwegian nationals, this should be done.

In regard to actual implements of warfare, such as airplanes, tanks, artillery, trucks, and radar equipment, we shall be lucky if we realize a billion dollars on what may represent an expenditure of some $20 billion to $25 billion. There should be no sale of such material to private dealers and care must be taken, furthermore, lest arms and munitions acquired in this fashion become a source of international disturbance.[1]

Only an arbitrary estimate can be made of the recoverable value of industrial materials and products and foodstuffs furnished under lend-lease. In this category come such diverse things as machine tools and equipment used in British industry, stocks of foodstuffs, textiles, and materials of all sorts, including copper, aluminum, and steel products. Goods and materials of this kind will be in almost every conceivable location and possession. Machine tools furnished to the British government, for example, will often have been installed in privately owned factories. Some of these machine tools will be useful for peacetime production. Others are exclusively for purposes of war.[2]

[1] For example, a sale of arms to some Latin American power, say Argentina, might disturb seriously the balance of power in South America.

[2] At the beginning of 1945 Great Britain paid $31.5 million, the agreed-upon depreciated value, to acquire title to about 58,000 machine tools provided under lend-lease. The original cost of the tools was $166 million, although part of

Lend-lease deliveries of such goods and materials may represent outlays of $12 billion; of this we might recover a billion dollars. A considerable portion of unused foodstuffs and textiles might be sold to UNRRA. Ships delivered to our Allies under lend-lease should be dealt with as a special category. We should require the return to the United States government of all still afloat. Some or most of the merchant ships might be sold to the countries that have received them under lend-lease. The disposal of lend-lease merchant ships must be governed primarily by our decisions with respect to our postwar mercantile marine,[1] and only secondarily by the policies determined upon for concluding lend-lease in general.

Where transportation facilities and airports have been installed, the United States government will have to negotiate separately with each country. In many instances we may have to accept whatever the other government is willing to pay, since the cost of dismantling and moving such installations is usually prohibitive.

The United States government would naturally retain or acquire title to factories constructed here for lend-lease purposes. The original cost of such factories may be in the neighborhood of $750 million. The factors determining their recoverable value will be the same as those affecting like plants built as part of our own defense program. Some $250 million might be recovered.

On the basis of the rough estimates and guesses we might expect to recoup a total of some $2 billion or $3 billion out of a possible total expenditure of as much as $40 billion or $50 billion.

HOW IS LEND-LEASE TO BE REPAID?

If repayments under lend-lease amount to some $2 billion or $3 billion, in what form and under what terms might

---

this sum represented the cost of machine tools sunk in transit (*The New York Times*, January 26, 1945).

[1] See Chap. VII.

repayment be made? If our prospective balance of payments were to be passive, that is, were we likely to purchase a greater net total of goods and services than we would sell during the postwar period, we might well require cash repayment over a reasonably short period. However, our balance of payments, at least in the immediate postwar period, will be quite the reverse. Moreover, the balance-of-payments position of most debtor countries is likely to be particularly weak during this period. Consequently, payments of even $2 billion or $3 billion might present serious difficulties.

One feasible settlement would involve a "grace period" of five years during which no payments would be required and no interest charged. At the end of that time, a program of amortization, with reasonable interest charges, could be initiated. Payment would also be facilitated by our acceptance of strategic materials, supplies of which might be deficient here in case of war. Such things as manganese and tungsten could thus be added to a "security stock pile."

This type of settlement would mean that we charged nothing for lend-lease aid rendered our Allies during the war. Lend-lease would have added as much as $40 billion or $50 billion to our national debt. We would have to pay interest on this sum. At an interest rate of 2 per cent, this might mean paying as much as $1 billion per year in additional taxes on account of lend-lease—not to mention amortization.

There is no way that this cost can be avoided. If we try to obtain much larger amounts from our Allies in repayment, we might be able to negotiate a more favorable paper settlement, but if the analogy of the inter-Allied debts of the last war furnishes any criterion, this would only mean carrying a doubtful asset on our books. All argument supports a settlement in which we would neither play the role of Santa Claus nor expose ourselves to the charge of playing Shylock—with no more profit from the part than the original Shylock received.

VII. OUR MERCANTILE MARINE POLICY

BY THE end of the war with Germany and Japan we may have a merchant fleet of some 60 million deadweight tons, *i.e.*, around 60 per cent of the world's total tonnage of merchant ships.[1] In 1939 about 12 million deadweight tons or 8 million gross tons, some 15 per cent of total world tonnage, was under our flag.[2] Our share of the total world merchant tonnage has increased at this phenomenal rate during the war partly because the tonnage of some of the other countries whose fleets carried the bulk of international trade before the war has been so seriously reduced. The merchant fleet of the United Kingdom, for example, had declined from some

---

[1] World shipping may reach a total of as much as 100 million deadweight tons by the end of 1945 as compared with an aggregate for all countries in 1939 of some 80 or 85 million deadweight tons.

[2] Twelve million deadweight tons is an approximation which includes a considerable amount of obsolescent tonnage. This estimate includes ships in coastwise and intercoastal trade but excludes shipping on the Great Lakes and on internal waterways. In addition, American parent companies owned around 2 million deadweight tons that were operated under foreign registries. Only some 4 to 5 million tons were actually engaged in *foreign* trade. The *Statistical Yearbook of the League of Nations*, 1939–1940, p. 181, gives the tonnage of merchant ships of 100 tons or more for the United States as 11,939,000 *gross* tons. This includes tonnage on the Great Lakes. (Some sources give lower totals. *Lloyd's Register of Ships* places United States tonnage in 1939 at 8,909,892 gross tons.) The world total is given by this source as 69,440,000 gross tons. This also includes coastal shipping of the various countries.

It is difficult to obtain statistics that are comparable between countries and between different dates. Data are given in several different types of tons, of which the most common are gross tons and deadweight tons. Ordinarily, a deadweight ton is the equivalent of about two-thirds of a gross ton. But reconciling the differences in tonnage estimates by any simple arithmetical adjustment proves to be impracticable. Statistics based on different minima are also a source of confusion. Some sources list ships over 100 gross tons, others over 1,000, and still others above 2,000.

26 million deadweight tons to about 20 million deadweight tons by the end of 1943[1] but has since increased somewhat.

Should we plan to operate our tremendously expanded tonnage under our own flag after the war? What would be the advantages and disadvantages of doing so? If we do not operate this great fleet ourselves, what should we do with it? These are some of the questions that arise.

National security must be the foremost consideration. We came perilously close to losing the war during the worst of the submarine crisis. To ensure against a shipping shortage that might once again threaten our national existence, we must maintain the minimum merchant tonnage dictated by military considerations. Unfortunately, we cannot know with any great accuracy what minimum tonnage is needed to ensure that shipping will not be our Achilles heel in some future war.[2] We do not know whether we shall be involved in war during the next decades or, if so, what countries we shall be fighting. If the peace agreement does not itself carry seeds of a new war, and if an international organization for the adjudication of disputes and the prevention of armed aggression is successfully established, the size of the mercantile fleet required for reasonable national security may be rela-

---

[1] British ocean-going shipping amounted to about 17.5 million gross tons at the beginning of the present war and had shrunk to about 13.5 million gross tons by the end of 1943 (*Statistics Relating to the War Effort of the United Kingdom*, Cmd. 6564, His Majesty's Stationery Office, London, 1944). Since then, however, construction has exceeded sinkings. Canadian construction has also increased.

[2] In a sense it is unreal to deal with this problem by estimating the optimum size of the postwar fleet. Actually, the present laws governing the size of the fleet will be amended or some act or series of acts will be passed, which will make it more or less profitable to build merchant ships in the United States and to operate them under our flag. The profitability of operation will depend primarily upon the volume of trade to be carried and the degree of foreign competition. Consequently, it is not possible to determine just what amount of shipping we shall be able to operate. Nevertheless, it is of some point to estimate the minimum size required from the standpoint of national defense. Such an estimate would be useful in preparing the legislation needed to maintain that minimum at the least national expense.

tively small. Within five or ten years after hostilities cease we might have a better idea of these matters; for the time being, it is not expedient to settle upon a long-term national policy. We must, however, decide upon a temporary policy for the immediate postwar years.

In contrast to the arguments based on national security, purely economic arguments in favor of a large American merchant marine are not impressive. Still, economic arguments do exist in favor of maintaining a fairly sizable fleet. The first of these is that a country needs at least a nuclear merchant marine to protect it against exploitation by shipping monopolies of other countries. In reality, the sharp competition between foreign merchant marines for the profit to be gained by carrying our merchandise, which characterized prewar foreign trade, weakens this contention. Another rather valid argument is that the maintenance of an American merchant marine, with the help of federal subsidies, served our exporters by establishing shipping lines between American and foreign ports, which otherwise would not have been operated. Still, it remains true that the strength of the case for the maintenance of an American merchant marine by means of government subsidies rests chiefly on national security.

In view of the uncertainty of national-security requirements, why not simply retain and operate the present gigantic tonnage so as to have the greatest possible margin of safety? The answer is that it would be expensive to do so. We could hire most of our shipping more cheaply than we could ship for ourselves. Construction of ships in American yards requires large subsidies if our higher construction costs are to be covered. Operating them with high-priced American labor under the American flag necessitates smaller but still considerable subsidies. For existing ships the construction subsidies have been paid already; but when these ships have to be replaced, new subsidies will be needed. To pay the American level of sailors' wages and to provide proper living conditions, substantial operating subsidies have been required, but these have rightly been considered part of the cost of national security.[1]

If no other employment were available for the men who operate these ships, it might well pay us, even from the economic point of view, to bear the cost of the necessary subsidies. In reality, however, our operation of a huge merchant marine would probably mean that the funds available to other countries, and particularly to Great Britain, for the purchase of American goods would be less by the amount we would have paid them for hauling our goods. For every ton of goods shipped in American instead of British vessels the British would have less funds to purchase, for example, American tobacco. *If we could haul the goods more cheaply than the British, this would of course constitute no argument against our operating as large a merchant marine as was profitable. If, however, we can increase our national income by producing, say, cotton and automobiles for the British, who would pay for them by carrying our goods, then within the limits of our national security we should do so—especially if British shipping is likely to be available to us during a possible war.*[2]

The operation of a merchant marine much larger than our prewar fleet would have an adverse effect upon the international balance of payments of Great Britain, Norway, Greece, Sweden, and the Netherlands, countries that have depended greatly upon income from shipping. In 1937, an unusually good year for both our domestic production and our foreign trade, we paid $130 million more for foreign shipping services than we received from foreigners for our

[1] In spite of subsidies and other aids to American shipping under the Merchant Marine Act of 1928 and of 1936, the proportion of American trade carried in our own vessels declined steadily. Thus, by 1939, we carried in our own bottoms not more than 30 per cent of our imports and less than 20 per cent of our exports. In 1939 only 23 per cent of our ocean-going tonnage was engaged in foreign commerce, compared with 61 per cent in 1920 and 39 per cent in 1930 (Hal B. Lary and Associates, *The United States in World Economy*, Economic Series 23, United States Department of Commerce, Bureau of Foreign and Domestic Commerce, Washington, D.C., 1943, p. 73).

[2] The same argument runs, of course, against all forms of subsidy and tariff.

shipping. This sum was large enough, when added to all other services and goods received in payment from foreigners, to pay for the goods and services we furnished foreigners in that year and thus bring about an approximate equilibrium in our balance of payments.[1] Comparing these $130 million, for example, with the $369 million representing the value of raw cotton exports in the same year, also a year of abnormally high exports of cotton, we may say that roughly one-third of our 1937 cotton exports was paid for by the net value of shipping services rendered to the United States by foreign merchant fleets.

However, in 1938, a very bad year from the standpoint of domestic production, exports, and earnings of merchant ships, we paid only $36 million net for foreign shipping services. This amount would have paid for not more than one-sixth of the $229 million worth of raw cotton exported that year.[2]

The merchant marine services of the United Kingdom produced in the prewar period somewhat more than £100 million annually, which was one means of payment for the large excess of imports over exports in British trade with the United States. Since, at best, the postwar British balance of payments is bound to be difficult, the loss of any substantial part of this sum as a result of competition with the American merchant marine would be a serious matter. The same is true, in varying degrees, with respect to the Norwegian, the Swedish, and other merchant marines.[3]

---

[1] *The United States in World Economy*, Table I, United States Balance of International Payments, 1919–1939. This amount of $130 million was, however, only about 4 per cent of the value of either our imports or our exports for 1937.

[2] Data on cotton exports are from "Summary of Foreign Trade of the United States, Calendar Year 1940," *International Reference Service*, United States Department of Commerce, Bureau of Foreign and Domestic Commerce, Vol. I, No. 67 (December, 1941).

[3] Net shipping receipts in 1937, expressed as a percentage of receipts from exports, have been estimated at 13.4 per cent for the United Kingdom, 36.5 per cent for Norway, 9.2 per cent for the Netherlands, 5.9 per cent for Sweden, and 24.1 per cent for Greece. The same figure for the United States was only 1.9 per cent. See John S. Smith, "World Income from Shipping," *Foreign Com-*

It might be argued that there will be so much cargo after the war that American shippers could operate a greatly expanded merchant marine without taking business away from countries that were leaders in shipping before the war. World tonnage by the end of 1945 might be estimated as around 100 million deadweight tons. Certainly there will not be an oversupply of shipping in relation to cargo for at least two years after the end of the war in Europe. All the space available will be needed for relief shipments, for replenishing of depleted inventories, and the requirements of demobilization and of armies of occupation.

When the extreme need for shipping in the immediate postwar period subsides, there will be a surplus shipping tonnage unless a large expansion in world trade takes place. This does not mean, however, that there will be a surplus of particular types of ships for specialized shipping or a surplus of the faster, more efficient vessels.

The prospect is good that world trade will expand in the decade after the war to levels substantially beyond those of 1939. Wartime experience has proved conclusively that the volume of peacetime industrial production in the United States could be increased to an amount greatly above that of 1939. Indeed, there is general agreement in the United States that these potentialities must be realized. A similar attitude prevails in Great Britain, in spite of the fact that the possible increase in their industrial production over 1939 is apparently not nearly so great. As a matter of fact, this determination to enlarge production, coupled with the ability to do so, exists in varying degrees throughout the world. If the International Monetary Fund and the International Bank for Reconstruction and Development are approved, and if their resources are added to the employable gold holdings and dollar balances available elsewhere, it appears that global

---

merce Weekly, April 29, 1944. In other words, for all countries listed except the United States, the earnings of the merchant marine were an important source for import payments.

credit resources should be fairly adequate for financing such an expansion of production.[1]   Should the potential increase in world production be achieved even partially, no serious long-term oversupply in world shipping need result from the abnormal rate of shipbuilding during the war.

Whatever the total amount of world shipping, there still remains the problem of what nations should own and operate the shipping.   Around 60 per cent of world tonnage may be in American hands after the war as compared with around 15 per cent before the war.   The economic arguments against increasing our share of international shipping over the prewar level have been examined.   If we increase our share, we reduce the potential foreign purchases of American goods and pay unnecessarily heavy charges for the transporting of our goods in international trade.

How, then, are the conflicting factors of economic advantage and national security to be reconciled?   There can be no simple compromise, especially as only the roughest estimate can be made of the minimum which national security demands.[2]

The experience of this war has demonstrated that ships laid up as long as twenty years can be reconditioned for practical

[1] Serious balance-of-payments problems would still exist, however, for certain countries.   Also, the optimistic prospect of world trade expansion might fail of realization.   The danger of a great world-wide depression has by no means been eliminated.   Intelligence and dynamic action by the various national governments will be required to provide the volume of purchasing power necessary to take off the market all the goods that can be produced.   The return to a volume of output no greater than that of 1939 would mean the collapse of international economic cooperation.   If such circumstances are assumed, almost the whole set of postulates on which this study is based would be invalid.

[2] It will probably be smaller than some estimates assume.   It is perhaps not too great a simplification to say that, if we are called on to participate in another major war, we shall either do so as part of an alliance including Great Britain or we shall be conducting the defense of only this hemisphere.   Under the first set of circumstances, it would be almost as useful to our security to have a portion of the required ships in British hands as in our own.   In the second case, our need for ships might not be so great as in this war, in which our shipping needs have been caused so largely by the requirements of our Allies.

service as carriers of merchandise. Consequently, we could depend, at least in part, upon a laid-up reserve of ships to meet our requirements for national security.[1] An active tonnage of 12 million deadweight tons consisting of new, fast ships, kept in condition for continuous operation, plus a laid-up tonnage of perhaps 10 million tons rigidly restricted to war-time use only but capable of being put into service quickly, might represent a reasonable minimum provision for national security. Some expert opinion places the figure of active tonnage to be maintained at from 15 to 20 million tons.[2]

This seems small compared to the proposals of some shipping enthusiasts who are demanding a fleet large enough to carry 50 per cent or even 70 per cent of our foreign trade.[3]

[1] Perhaps as much as 2 million tons of our wartime merchant fleet may have to be kept in operation to meet routine needs of our navy after the war. A considerable portion of the special inactive defense reserve might consist of vessels whose conversion to peacetime uses from military and naval employment would be costly.

It has been estimated that ships can be laid up at an annual cost of from $3,000 to $5,000 per ship. The cost of laying up 1,500 ships for twenty years, therefore, might be estimated as $120 million. (By the middle of 1945 it will have cost from $15 billion to $17 billion to build our wartime fleet.) It would be essential that this laid-up fleet should be kept out of operation by statutory provisions, except in case of national emergency. Otherwise its existence would discourage new construction. This laid-up reserve might be scrapped partially or wholly at some future time if national security had been adequately ensured by other means.

[2] In a speech before the Mississippi Valley Association at St. Louis, Mo., November 27, 1944, Vice Admiral Land, Chairman of the United States Maritime Commission and War Shipping Administrator, expressed his opinion that "we can find use for 15 to 20 million deadweight tons of our fleet after the war ends." He suggested that peacetime requirements might be as follows.

For use in	Tons
Great Lakes shipping	3,500,000
River shipping	2,500,000
Coastal and intercoastal shipping	3,800,000
Foreign trade	7,500,000
Total	17,300,000

This was not, strictly speaking, an estimate of the minimum merchant tonnage required by considerations of national security.

[3] When it is advocated that a nation carry 50 per cent of its foreign trade or

Should a fleet no larger in total tonnage than our prewar merchant fleet but consisting largely of Victory or other modern, fast types of ships be kept in commission, its cargo and passenger-carrying capacity in coastal, internal, and foreign trade would substantially exceed that of our prewar merchant fleet. This would be true because so much of our pre-war merchant fleet was obsolescent or inactive for other reasons.

The current capacity of the shipbuilding yards that we would maintain in operation and our laid-up reserve should ensure us fairly well against the development of a sudden critical shortage of merchant ships that might threaten our national security. After providing for a laid-up reserve of some 10 million deadweight tons, some 35 million tons, the exact amount depending upon the duration of the war, would be available for other uses. There seems good reason why most of these ships, after American companies had been offered the opportunity for purchase, should be sold to countries among the United Nations that have lost heavily in tonnage during the war. These countries are Great Britain, Norway, Greece, the Netherlands, Denmark, France, Belgium, and Poland. Options on tonnage might be allotted to them in proportion to their net losses from the amount of their prewar tonnage. It is, of course, by no means certain that all these ships could be sold at reasonable prices. We should retain the most efficient ships for our own merchant marine. The least desirable of the remaining vessels might not bring much more than scrap value. It would be better to scrap such vessels than to demoralize the market by selling them.

---

50 per cent of both its exports and imports, in effect, this nation would be carrying *all* of its "share" of foreign trade.

Under certain assumptions as to types of ships, degree of utilization, turn-around time, volume of postwar trade, etc., the assumed 12 million deadweight tons might handle 50 per cent of our foreign trade and provide for coastwise and internal water transport as well. Under conditions that are likely to prevail, however, this tonnage would not provide for 50 per cent of our foreign trade plus coastwise and intercoastal trade.

This policy of selling to other United Nations the ships above the tonnage estimated to be necessary for our national security is not recommended as a matter of charity or justice. Its great advantage is that the countries purchasing these ships would the more quickly earn funds with which to purchase American goods. We would also avoid payment of the huge subsidies required to keep in operation, or in reserve, anything like all the ships we shall own at the end of the war.

We shall have to pay substantial subsidies to keep even the prewar tonnage of ships in operation.[1] We must be prepared to spend additional sums to maintain at least a minimum number of shipyards in production, since national security requires not only a merchant fleet but the means of expanding that fleet in an emergency. As long as the possibility of war persists, it would surely be inadvisable to permit loss of the know-how that we have acquired in shipbuilding.

The proposal that we sell a substantial portion of our merchant marine at the end of the war, while retaining the more efficient ships for our own operation and for a laid-up reserve, means taking a loss on the ships sold. We would be able to recover only a fraction of their actual cost. The loss, however, would be much less than that involved in retaining the entire fleet or attempting to operate a much larger proportion than that suggested.

There will remain the problem of obtaining payment for the ships sold to foreign countries. In some of the countries wishing to secure these ships, the balance-of-payments situation will be difficult. The greater the amount of shipping sold to these countries, however, the larger the amount of foreign exchange that they could earn from the services of

---

[1] It is possible that the higher costs for American-operated ships might be offset after the war by increases in wages and improvements in living conditions for crews of foreign merchant ships. It is also argued that if all laborsaving devices that are available could be utilized in American harbors and on American docks, our operating costs would not now be higher than those of other countries.

these ships, and the larger the sums available for meeting their obligations.

All the elements in our international trade policy are closely related. Our shipping policy is likely to be a substantial factor in determining the extent to which international economic cooperation will replace rigid national controls in the postwar world.

VIII. THE PROBLEM OF OUR NEW AND OVEREXPANDED WAR INDUSTRIES

How will the industries created by the war, or so enormously expanded as to constitute almost new industries, affect our foreign trade? The synthetic-rubber industry, the aluminum and magnesium industries, the machine-tool industry, the aviation industry—all face marketing problems on a really gigantic scale. Each of these industries now has a productive capacity greater than total domestic consumption before the war. Except for synthetic rubber, production is, in fact, several times the prewar domestic demand. In the case of synthetic rubber, the new production must compete with crude rubber from the plantations of Malaya and of the East Indies, the output of which, together with lesser amounts from other sources, was ample to supply world demand before synthetic rubber was produced in any appreciable quantities.

To these industries (except synthetic rubber) foreign trade is offered time and again as a sovereign remedy to relieve the affliction of excess capacity through "getting rid of the surplus abroad." Attempting to solve the problem of "overproduction" by selling abroad more than we are ready to buy is, of course, quite the ultimate in economic folly. The real potentialities of foreign trade as an outlet for these new-type industries will be determined, first, by our comparative advantage in such industries, which will determine how cheaply we can produce as compared with other countries; second, by the effect of trade restrictions and controls upon their sales abroad; and, finally, by the extent to which other countries are able to obtain dollar exchange through the sale of goods and services or through the floating of loans in our markets and the investment of American funds abroad. The relevant general principles have been discussed in previous chapters; the situation in which particular industries will find themselves is examined below.

SYNTHETIC-RUBBER INDUSTRY

By the end of the war, the total productive capacity of all types of synthetic-rubber plants in the United States may be as much as a million tons annually.[1] This total capacity is substantially greater than our total annual consumption of crude rubber before the war, which in the last "normal" year was around 600,000 tons. However, production-capacity figures in the case of synthetic rubber are deceptive. Such statistics do not differentiate between high-quality, high-cost, special-purpose synthetics, marketable even at prices triple that of crude rubber, and ordinary synthetic rubbers, which are not yet the equal of crude rubber in desirable qualities. These figures include both alcohol and petroleum synthetic-rubber plants and it is not yet certain which process will pass the test of cost and quality. Some of these plants may soon become obsolete as one process wins out over another for technical reasons or as price differentials change in the raw materials used.

There may well be a considerable export demand for some of the special-purpose synthetics, almost without regard to the cost of production. For the bulk of synthetic production, however, the question is not whether we can export but whether we should continue to produce for the domestic market or again import crude rubber from Malaya and the Dutch East Indies. If it turns out that we can manufacture a product comparable in quality to crude rubber, at a price as low as the cost of the imported natural material, synthetic-rubber production for the domestic market will cease to be

[1] See the very useful study by K. E. Knorr, *Rubber after the War*, Food Research Institute, Stanford University, California, 1944, p. 7, which estimated 1 million tons, including a very small amount of Canadian production. This estimate was confirmed by Secretary of Commerce Jesse Jones in a press release of January 17, 1945.

problematical.[1] In that case, however, a serious balance-of-payments problem might arise for those countries that depended upon their sales of crude rubber to us to furnish the means for their purchase of imports—but that is another story.

It is quite possible that by the end of the war with Japan and by the time crude rubber is again available, we shall be producing ordinary grades of synthetic rubber as cheaply as crude rubber can be imported. If we are not able to do so by that time, the question will arise as to whether tariff protection or government subsidy should be provided to assure continuation of the industry on a large scale. As is the case with our large new merchant marine, the primary factor to be considered is national security. It is impossible to foresee exactly what economic sacrifices are warranted in the interest of national security. Until the political scene is greatly clarified, it is not likely that American public opinion will tolerate abandoning the synthetic-rubber industry.

Consequently, whether or not we should provide protection or subsidy for the synthetic-rubber industry is not the basic question. The real question is: how much of the industry should be maintained and if it is necessary to protect it com-

---

[1] In a press release of January 17, 1945, Secretary of Commerce Jesse Jones stated that synthetic rubber was being produced in some plants at less than 18 and 20 cents per pound. But the average cost of production was 33 cents per pound because 60 per cent of production was being carried on in high-cost plants using alcohol.

For Buna S, the best all-purpose synthetic, a postwar price of from 12 to 35 cents per pound had earlier been forecast. Colonel Bradley Dewey stated in December, 1943, that Buna S was being manufactured at less than 14 cents per pound. (This included management fees but did not include depreciation. Whether or not any interest on the investment was included was not stated.) It has been claimed that large-scale plants, working at capacity and using the petroleum process, will be able to produce butadiene at from 8 to 9 cents per pound, provided by-products can be utilized to advantage. If grain alcohol is used the cost will be much higher.

Natural rubber, on the other hand, has ranged from an average price of 3.4 cents per pound during the depression of 1933 to 19.4 cents in 1937. Over the entire period the average was 12.1 cents per pound (Knorr, *op. cit.*).

petitively, should this be by tariff or government subsidy? Informed opinion probably favors subsidies over tariff protection, on the ground that subsidies can be more easily withdrawn. However, our recent political controversies over subsidies to farmers, consumers, air lines, shipping, etc., has somewhat dimmed the allure of subsidies as a substitute for tariffs.

It is not possible to gauge the amount of subsidy or tariff protection necessary to keep a substantial portion of the synthetic-rubber industry in production—if, indeed, either is required. The amount will be affected both by new technological developments and by changes in costs of petroleum (which we may sometime import on a large scale). Likewise, it may depend upon whether alcohol is obtained from grains or from some other source. If grain alcohol is used, its cost will depend upon whether or not it is sold to the rubber industry as a "surplus" commodity, in lieu of subsidizing grain exports or of paying farmers not to raise grain.

ALUMINUM AND MAGNESIUM

Domestic productive capacity for aluminum has increased five- or sixfold.[1] Our exports of manufactured aluminum products had already reached considerable proportions before the war. These facts suggest that aluminum may well bulk large in our postwar export trade. Our competitive position will be strengthened by the damage that has occurred to the aluminum industry in Germany, in Russia, and elsewhere in Europe; but continued expansion in our sales of aluminum products abroad will depend primarily upon other factors, since this loss of productive capacity abroad can be expected to be temporary. Maximum export possibilities depend upon accelerated industrialization throughout the world, requiring increased amounts of the light metals, and upon the successful

---

[1] Domestic production of aluminum in 1939, at some 90 per cent of capacity, was about 450 million pounds. Present capacity has been estimated to be around 2.7 billion pounds annually.

achievement of full employment at least in the major countries. Nevertheless, domestic consumption of aluminum will probably continue to be much larger than exports.

The same general situation that characterizes the aluminum industry seems to hold true for magnesium, only more so. Domestic production has increased phenomenally, from less than 7 million pounds to over 400 million pounds. Magnesium is an even "newer" metal than aluminum, as far as its large-scale industrial uses are concerned. Its domestic market is likely to be more important than its export market. Competition, particularly with German production, may be severe.

The future of international trade in aluminum and magnesium, both highly cartelized, may be greatly influenced by postwar national and international policies in regard to cartels.

AIRPLANES

In no other among our abnormally expanded industries do we have the international production leadership that we have in aviation. Not only will our plane production far exceed that of any other country, but our capacity will be concentrated in the production of transport planes or allied types. The pilots of all the United Nations have become familiar with the operation of American planes. Peoples of all countries are accustomed to seeing American planes and are familiar with their extraordinary record of performance. Even the past achievements of our automobile industry serve as a foundation for the prestige of the American plane.

At the close of the war, only Great Britain and Soviet Russia will be in any position to compete with us in production of planes; and it seems unlikely that the latter will be a serious competitor. Other demands on Russia's economy and alternative uses for the resources now employed in the production of planes will be very urgent.

When peace comes, the United States government probably

will possess more surplus transport planes than would be needed to meet all the requirements of all the air lines in the world. Furthermore, these planes are surprisingly long-lived. If they were sold to commercial airlines without any conditions as to length of use, some would undoubtedly be in operation ten years later. Replacement demand for the first five or six years would be very small. Under such circumstances, technology in the production of new types of planes might become frozen. It might, therefore, be better to lease such planes for a term of, say, three years. In this way a considerable gap in demand, and consequently in technical progress, might be avoided.[1]

No matter how favorable our competitive position, it will not enable us to keep in plane production anything beyond a small fraction of the resources now so used. Our export sales can be expected only to supplement our domestic sales, and both together cannot hope to keep employed facilities that nothing short of the fabulous demand of war could have brought into existence.

MACHINE TOOLS

The manifold increase in our capacity for machine-tool production raises problems not unlike those of aluminum and magnesium, except that the product is much more diversified and American leadership in this field of production is more pronounced.[2] The industries of Great Britain and Soviet Russia and, to some extent, those of other nations have been equipped partially with American-made machine tools, largely by means of lend-lease. This might be supposed to have glutted these markets. Actually, the nations of the world have become acquainted with American-made machine tools as never before. German production and competition

---

[1] It is emphatically *not* recommended that the planes be lend-leased.

[2] In 1939 the machine-tool industry, operating at less than half capacity, manufactured a product valued at $200 million. At peak production in 1942, the value amounted to $1⅓ billion. Currently it is operating again substantially below capacity.

in this field is likely to be reduced by bomb damage and other war causes and may be curtailed by the peace terms, even while a substantial amount of re-equipping of European industry will be required. To a greater extent even than in the case of aluminum, magnesium, or airplanes, the immediate market will probably be determined by the flow of funds for long-term investment.

All our abnormally extended industries have a special stake in international trade expansion, although their competitive position in world trade is as yet uncertain. As with all other export industries, the successful development of national programs of full employment and international cooperation to achieve freer trade would benefit them most.

IX. PROSPECTIVE TRENDS IN OUR FOREIGN TRADE

THE IMMEDIATE POSTWAR PROSPECT

THE prospects of a strong demand for American exports are excellent for the first couple of years after the close of the war. Our capacity to supply that demand, and how quickly it will be sated, will depend upon the duration of the war with Japan after the defeat of Germany. We may expect the abnormal demand attributable directly to the war to taper off within a year or two after all hostilities cease, assuming that the Japanese phase of the war lasts about a year after victory over Germany is won.

This "abnormal" export demand will be caused by the depleted inventories of goods in all countries and at all stages of production, from the primary producer through the wholesaler and the retailer to the ultimate consumer. It is not to be expected, however, that these inventories will be replenished to peacetime levels during the year or two of anticipated rush demand for American exports. Many European countries will defer completing their stock piles until they can obtain at least part of their requirements from domestic sources.

Not only are inventories at all points of production seriously depleted, but industrial facilities in most of Europe will have been seriously damaged by air bombardment or other military action, by "scorched earth" policies, by sabotage, and possibly by civil disturbances after military defeat. Industrial equipment will have depreciated owing to lack of adequate repairs and to operation by unskilled labor, in addition to ordinary wear and tear.

In consequence, there will be an enormous demand for commodities of widely differing types and categories, from foodstuffs, clothing, and all kinds of consumer goods to industrial raw materials, railroad and automotive equipment, public-utility installations, and almost every sort of capital equipment.

There will be a considerable export demand for our agricultural products during the first year or two after the war—but how long this demand will continue is uncertain. It is difficult for Americans to realize how far European countries had progressed toward agricultural self-sufficiency before the war. This attempt at agricultural self-sufficiency may continue after the war. During the war the shortage of foodstuffs in Europe was not so severe as was generally supposed, even though it has now become acute. Consequently, we may experience an agricultural-surplus problem in the United States some time during the first two or three years of the peace.[1] Serious surpluses probably will be confined to wheat and cotton, unless we come to a severe economic depression, in which case we might also have burdensome supplies of meat and dairy products.

The temporary excessive demand will not all stem from Europe. In spite of large resources in gold and dollar exchange, Latin American countries have been unable to purchase all that they wanted from the United States. A good deal of this deferred demand will enter the market during the first peacetime year. Some of it can be met by British and Swedish firms almost at once; other European producers will find their way into the market at an accelerated rate during the early postwar years.

Evidence indicates that, to finance these purchases, there will be fairly adequate resources of gold and dollar balances in the hands of countries that were either neutral or nonbelligerent or did not take an active part in the war. It has

---

[1] However, the most pressing problems of agricultural surpluses would tend to disappear if substantially full employment were attained and if agricultural prices are not kept at levels unduly stimulating to production, and with a differential between world and domestic prices that does not permit our stocks to be cleared by foreign demand.

been estimated that total holdings of gold and dollar balances of all types by foreign countries are now two or three times as large as they were at the close of World War I. This estimate may be excessive, but that large resources of this type exist is a certainty. Of course, all these funds will not be used for the purchase of goods and services from the United States. However, Sweden, Switzerland, Turkey, Portugal, most Latin American countries, and some others should have little difficulty in financing their purchases in the United States during the initial years after the war.[1]

This does not mean that there will be no problem of postwar balance of payments; quite the contrary. But the balance of payments will not present a serious transition problem for the countries at the moment well supplied with gold and other employable foreign exchange. On the other hand, several important countries will experience serious difficulties in finding means of payment for much-needed imports during the first postwar years.

The United Kingdom stands in the forefront of countries that will be faced with the problem of how to pay for commodities and equipment required for postwar rehabilitation. The combined loss of export trade, liquidation of foreign investments, damage to overseas possessions through enemy occupation, bomb damage, and accumulation of a huge indebtedness in blocked sterling will not make matters easy for the British. Direct or indirect assistance through the International Monetary Fund and the International Bank for Reconstruction and Development would afford some aid in solving this problem. It seems that British commercial-credit standing is strong enough to supplement these resources; still, the problem may require special measures for its solution.

Soviet Russia, too, apart from her long-term requirements, will need large sums to reconstruct her devastated regions and to restore her peacetime economy during the first couple of years after the war. The resources of the International

[1] See pp. 50–53 for a fuller discussion of this point.

Monetary Fund and of the International Bank would take care of a portion of these needs. So great will be the military and political prestige of Soviet Russia after the war that she is likely to find little difficulty in obtaining considerable export credits from Europe's industrial countries.

Unquestionably, an even stronger demand for American exports would exist in the early postwar era, and such demand would continue for a longer period, were additional large loans offered by the United States to countries whose gold resources and dollar balances will not be sufficient to satisfy their desires for American commodities. Before any such loans are made, however, we must make sure how they are to be repaid or serviced. If we are not able or willing to accept goods and services in repayment at some future date, we shall have given away, in effect, the goods and services financed by such loans. If we are to sustain demand for American products by giving away funds for their purchase, we should consider the claims, say, of southern sharecroppers along with those of, let us say, the Patagonians.

After the war with Germany ends, the immediate problem will be less one of export demand than one of export supply. Certainly, we shall be unable for some months to supply both domestic and export demand for all kinds of goods. We shall not be able to meet all demand for some goods, for example, automobiles, for perhaps as long as two years.

Our wartime restrictions on foreign trade should be removed as soon as possible. At least for some months, however, it may be necessary to resort to quantitative export restrictions and controls, in order to avoid a disorderly scramble for goods. In an unregulated scramble for scarce goods, countries with the largest cash balances would have an unfair advantage. The inflationary effects of such a scramble could be serious. Removal of all controls over exports and over the expenditures of foreign balances in this country might spur a temporary sharp rise in prices similar to the post-Armistice boom after World War I. The proper time for the relaxation and later for the removal of such controls should not be decided without reference to domestic economic conditions.

LONG-TERM TRENDS
The Factual Background

At the height of world prosperity in 1929, we were the world's leading exporters, providing 15.6 per cent of the total world exports, while we received 12.2 per cent of the world total of imports. The United States at that time accounted for 39 per cent of the total raw material and foodstuff consumption of the fifteen most important commercial nations.[1] These percentages declined somewhat during the great depression and had not fully recovered when the present war began; yet, the United States remained the most dynamic and significant factor in world economy.

Foreign trade is important to our national economy, although there is some tendency to exaggerate its role. In 1929 our foreign trade amounted to some 8 per cent of our national income. During 1937, 1938, and 1939, the percentage was about 6.[2]

More than 70 per cent of all our imports of goods consisted of materials used in further production. Another 8 or 9 per cent

---

[1] Some of the data upon which this chapter is based were taken from Hal B. Lary and Associates, *The United States in World Economy*, Economic Series 23, United States Department of Commerce, Bureau of Foreign and Domestic Commerce, Washington, D.C., 1943, and from August Maffry and Hal B. Lary, *Foreign Trade after the War*, Economic Series 28, United States Department of Commerce, Bureau of Foreign and Domestic Commerce, Washington, D.C., 1943. Conclusions drawn from these and other data often differ, however, from those of the authors of the works cited.

[2] In 1937, for example, our imports of goods amounted to $3,084 million, and our exports to $3,349 million. Adding the value of "imported" services (shipping, capital services, etc.) to merchandise imports brings the total to $4,520 million. A similar addition to exports brings that total to $4,489 million. This was our most prosperous year after the depression and before the present war, when both exports and imports were unusually high, reflecting the high national income of that year, $71,456 million. The low ratio of our foreign trade to national income is due in part to the effect of our protective tariff.

It is easy to compute the ratio of imports or exports to national income, each

included fats and oils and fuels and lubricants, and about 10 or 11 per cent were foodstuffs. Finished consumers' goods, other than foodstuffs, represented less than 6 per cent of the total imports.[1]

For many years our total annual import of goods has tended to be much less than our exports of goods. In 1939, for example, our imports amounted to roughly $2,318 million and our exports to $3,177 million.[2] Even after allowing for "invisible imports" of services such as shipping, tourist expenditures, and insurance, normally larger than our "invisible exports," the tendency toward an export surplus continued.

Factors Causing Changes in the Volume of Our Foreign Trade

Long-time trends in our foreign trade tend to be obscured by alternations of prosperity and depression in the domestic economy. The year-to-year changes in the volume of our imports are closely correlated with the year-to-year changes in the volume of our industrial production. The correlation is inescapable as long as a very large proportion of our imports are raw materials for our industry.[3]

The volume of our imports appears to vary little with changes in the prices of these imports. Apparently this is

---

of which was about 6 per cent in 1937. But how much did this "swapping" of about $4.5 billion of exports for imports of about the same amount add to our national real income? That is difficult to answer.

If there were any possibility of our failing to obtain important raw materials for essential production because of an inability to exchange exports for imports, the loss would be very great. Should we fail to exchange, for example, commodities such as wheat for commodities like cotton textiles, we would experience a loss due to the fact that we would be employing some of our resources, by assumption more efficient in producing wheat, to the manufacture of cotton textiles. If for a similar reason we were unable to procure such consumers' goods as coffee, there would be a notable loss in what might be termed "intangible income," *i.e.*, satisfactions desired by our citizenry for its earnings.

[1] These data are for the years 1935–1937. See *Foreign Trade after the War.*

[2] "Summary of Foreign Trade of the United States, Calendar Year 1940," *International Reference Service*, United States Department of Commerce, Bureau of Foreign and Domestic Commerce, Vol. I, No. 67 (December, 1941), pp. 6, 9.

[3] See *The United States in World Economy*, pp. 37–39.

also due to the preponderance in our imports of materials used in further production. When business is booming, large amounts of these goods are imported almost regardless of price. During an economic depression, lower prices on these imported materials are not a sufficient inducement to manufacturers to enlarge their output and, consequently, their imports of component materials.

Statistical evidence on the subject is inconclusive, but some data suggest that changes in our tariff structure in the period between the two world wars did not have a major effect upon the volume of our imports.[1] No doubt, this reflects to some extent the fact that our tariff was high enough to keep competitive imports out even before the tariff acts of 1921, 1922, and 1930, and that the tariff cuts under the Reciprocal Trade Agreements Acts were not sufficient to destroy the protection enjoyed by the commodities included in the agreements.

PROBABLE FUTURE TRENDS IN EXPORTS

Manufactures

One of the trends most likely to continue is the increasing proportion of manufactured products as compared to agricultural products in our total exports. For the years 1901–1905, the average yearly export of agricultural products was 61 per cent of the yearly export total, while nonagricultural products accounted for 39 per cent of the total. In 1939 agricultural exports had fallen to 21 per cent and nonagricultural products had risen to 79 per cent.[2] This trend largely represents our industrial coming of age. For example, machinery and automotive vehicles, two of the important classifications in our finished-product exports, steadily gained in proportion to our total exports through the depression of the 1930's and on through the period of recovery.

[1] See *ibid.*, p. 54, for a discussion of this point.
[2] "Summary of Foreign Trade of the United States, Calendar Year 1940," Table 15, p. 23.

The prospects for a continued growth in such exports are very good. The process of industrialization of "backward" countries holds promise of great demand for capital goods. Demand for American manufactured goods may continue strong even in European countries. We have a competitive advantage in the production of heavy machinery, machine tools, and other commodities fabricated by mass-production methods or requiring large investments in fixed capital. Our extensive domestic market makes possible the production of those commodities on a large scale and at low cost, placing us in a favorable position for entering the export market. Few countries have such favorable conditions and possess also the engineering and managerial skills and the experience necessary to compete seriously with us in this type of production. Of these countries, at least one, Germany, will hardly be in a position to compete for some years.

As in the production of capital goods, we have an advantage in the manufacturing techniques of a whole range of consumer commodities, such as automobiles, electric refrigerators, motion pictures, etc. These are a type of goods closely associated with the whole trend of development of modern urban, industrialized society. Beyond our know-how in the technical production of such goods, we have developed— again, first in our home market—the advertising and selling skills that build demand for these goods here and elsewhere. It is no small advantage to the sale of such consumer durables that almost universally the American way of life is looked upon as the most advanced in urban industrialized living. But, whereas the capital goods mentioned have a high order of priority as a charge to the foreign-exchange balances of any country that has exchange control, the second category of commodities is most likely to be excluded under exchange control. Consequently, industries producing such commodities have a particular interest in the removal or reduction of exchange control.

Agricultural Products

The decline in the value of our agricultural exports was already well under way before the war. Our wheat exports had dwindled until wheat moved out only sporadically and then with the aid of export subsidies. This was caused in part by the Agricultural Adjustment Administration's program of limiting wheat production; in part the decline in demand reflects the lack of dollar exchange with which foreign countries might have purchased our agricultural products. This, in turn, goes back to some extent to our own tariff and the limited sales in our domestic markets of the manufactures of countries that otherwise might have bought our wheat.

At the same time, almost every European country introduced programs aimed at agricultural self-sufficiency. These were not simply the reaction to our foreign trade policy; they reflected the autarchical ideas of Fascist regimes as well as a growing fear of war.

From another point of view, the decline in our agricultural exports reflects the unwillingness of the American farmer, conscious of the comparatively high wages paid in American industry, to accept prices sufficiently low to compete in the world market.

It is probable that under conditions of substantially full employment and a national income of $140 billion our wheat production would not, over good and bad crop years, greatly exceed domestic consumption, unless the price to the farmer is maintained at uneconomically high levels. Average annual production would hardly run much in excess of 800 million bushels per year.[1] This seems the more likely when alternative employment opportunities for farm workers under the assumed conditions of a high level of industrial activity are taken into account. Domestic consumption, running at a rate of around 700 million bushels per year before the war,

---

[1] The average production of the past two years (over 1 billion bushels) is far above the 1933–1942 average of 760 million bushels annually.

might closely approach or even equal domestic production after the war (not counting on the possible use of grain for synthetic rubber). Occasional wheat surpluses of from 100 to 200 million bushels may still present difficult technical problems if they are to be moved into the international market without price disturbances at home and abroad.

Estimates based on our wartime experience indicate that the quantities of meat consumed at a national income of $140 billion would leave little available for export. Indeed, some kinds of meat would have to be imported. Our meat exports, except for lard and bacon, had almost disappeared before the present war.[1] In 1937, our total exports of animals and their edible products amounted to no more than $43 million out of a total of $797 million for agricultural exports and out of a total of $3,349 million for all exports. Tobacco and cotton were still important exports in the 1930's. However, cotton exports had a distinctly downward trend. While average annual exports were 8.7 million bales in the period of 1925–1929, we exported about 4.5 million bales in 1938. American cotton accounted for only 20 per cent of foreign consumption in 1938, compared to 47 per cent in 1928. A fairly normal annual domestic production is about 13 million bales.[2] The highest domestic consumption during the present war reached well over 11 million bales, but it should be noted that large amounts for the Army and for lend-lease were included in what is called domestic consumption.

If national income were $140 billion and if cotton consumption maintained the same relation to national income as it did in 1937 (when national income was about $71.5 billion— the equivalent of $85.8 billion at 1944 prices—and cotton

[1] See *The United States in World Economy*, p. 61. See also "Summary of Foreign Trade of the United States, Calendar Year 1940," Table 15, p. 23.

[2] When prices are as high as at present, production remains as low as this "normal" only by means of acreage-reduction programs financed by the government. Average production has increased by over 100 pounds per acre during the last decade or so from a pre-New Deal average of about 175 pounds to the acre.

consumption was about 7.8 million bales), total consumption of cotton at home would be between 12 and 13 million bales. However, this ratio between national income and domestic use of cotton would hardly be maintained. A domestic market for some 10 million bales of cotton per year at an annual national income of $140 billion would not seem unlikely were it not for inroads made by the synthetic fibers. Their share of the cotton market may be enlarged, since now for the first time rayon and cotton fibers can compete directly on a price basis, owing to a steady decrease in the production costs of rayon fibers and to the present governmental policy of holding the price of cotton at parity.

However, significant technological developments that may lower the production cost of American cotton are now taking place. These developments affect not merely cotton picking but the sowing, the application of fertilizer, and the cultivating of cotton as well. After long delay, check planting and cross-row cultivation seem about to be utilized for cotton. The competitive position of American-grown cotton may therefore be considerably bettered during the postwar years.

At present American cotton can be sold abroad only with help of a considerable export subsidy. Indeed, import barriers are required to keep out Brazilian and other cotton currently selling on the world market substantially below the domestic price of American cotton. This situation presents a serious problem in any international program for lowering trade barriers and for eliminating interferences with freer international trade.

If we are to continue to market our agricultural products abroad by means of a two-price system, we should participate in the proposed Food and Agricultural Organization of the United Nations, along the lines proposed by the Hot Springs Conference in 1943, and in some form of international commodity organization. Ruthless world competition in subsidized exports of cotton and wheat would be a guaranteed source of international political rancor. If public funds are to be used to push our agricultural exports on foreign markets, they had far better appear in the form of lower prices to encourage increased consumption in low-income countries than as competitive export subsidies.

There is considerable reason to suppose that even if we succeed in maintaining the level of national income necessary to, and consistent with, reasonably full employment, our agricultural exports will continue their declining trend.[1] Should we have to import more agricultural products from abroad, a new political problem might develop, reversing the past situation. Farmers might become the effective proponents of protective tariffs while manufacturers might become advocates of lower tariffs.

TRENDS IN OUR IMPORTS
Consumers' Goods

It has been pointed out that the physical volume of our imports follows closely the changes in the volume of industrial production. The dominant factor is the large proportion of imports that are goods used in further production. Other than foodstuffs, finished consumers' goods are normally about 6 per cent of our imports.

It seems probable that finished consumers' goods will remain a small fraction of our imports compared to raw materials. However, should we achieve successful international cooperation for facilitating international trade, implemented by full-employment measures at home and abroad, the trend may change materially. The cumulative effect of

[1] Professor Theodore Schultz, in his report, *Agriculture in a Developing Economy*, prepared for the Committee for Economic Development, expresses the opinion that a serious surplus problem would remain in the case of both wheat and cotton even under conditions of full employment. A considerable export of agricultural products is envisaged in *Foreign Trade after the War*, Table II, A Hypothetical 7 Billion Dollar Export Trade, p. 18. It is estimated that at full employment, with a gross national product of $175 billion, in 1948 exports of raw cotton would have a value of $454 million—substantially greater than in 1937.

these favorable conditions might lead to still further lowering of trade barriers. The absorptive capacity of our domestic market for imported consumers' goods might be surprisingly large in such a setting.

Thus, it seems probable that at a high level of industrial production and with consequent high consumer income, the importing of luxury goods, such as handmade rugs, laces, *objets d'art*, etc., would materially increase. Likewise, if substantial cuts in our tariff were made, we could expect sizable increases in imports of other consumers' goods, such as clothing, leather goods, textiles, house furnishings, kitchenware, glassware, china, pottery, and notions. Increased expenditures for luxury items, like tourist expenditures, are especially useful in facilitating a satisfactory international balance of payments, in that they do not directly compete with domestic production. The domestic price structure is not disturbed nor is there a problem of transferring labor—consequences which may follow increased imports when they result from the removal of protective tariffs for commodities produced previously on a large scale domestically.

Tourist Expenditures

Assuming on the close of the war a hitherto unattained peacetime prosperity in the United States, such as would accompany reasonably full employment, expenditures by our tourists abroad might reach very high levels. The taste of foreign travel experienced by our soldiers and sailors (even if under most uncomfortable circumstances) plus the development of air transport may boost tourist expenditures from their 1929 level (estimated at almost $500 million) to an even more consequential place in the international balance of payments.

Raw Materials

Imports of certain raw materials may become larger than before the war, even if domestic employment is not increased.

Our zinc, lead, and copper resources have been seriously depleted by the demands of the war. The best grades of iron ores have likewise been depleted, and it is uncertain whether our petroleum reserves will be sufficient to meet our postwar needs. These reverses are somewhat offset by larger productive capacities in the light metals, aluminum and magnesium, and in plastics and new types of processed woods used as substitutes for metals. However, the tonnage of these possible substitutions is not great, and raw material for aluminum, bauxite, must in the main be imported.

With reasonably full employment within three or four years after the war, our imports of raw materials should increase tremendously over the period immediately preceding the war. In these circumstances it would be highly undesirable from the standpoint of conservation of our natural resources to continue protective tariffs upon minerals or other raw materials of which our supply is already running low.

GEOGRAPHICAL TRENDS

Europe

Outstanding among geographical trends has been the declining rank of Europe as a market for our exports and as a source of our imports. At the turn of the century, Europe was taking more than 75 per cent of our exports. By World War I, this percentage had fallen to 62 and by 1937–1939 to 41.[1] In 1938, our imports from Europe represented only about 29 per cent of the total.

By contrast, our exports to other countries of the Western Hemisphere more than doubled in the four decades from 1900 to the outbreak of the present war, and our exports to Asia and Oceania expanded by still greater percentages.[2]

[1] *The United States in World Economy*, p. 61.

[2] Arthur R. Upgren, in "Southeastern Asia and the Philippines as a Market," *The Annals of the American Academy of Political and Social Science*, Philadelphia, March, 1943, makes the percentage increase for the Western Hemisphere 270 per cent and for Asia and Oceania 550 per cent.

During the same period, our exports to Europe gained by only 30 per cent. In absolute terms, however, Europe remained still our most important consumer.

A striking characteristic of our trade with Europe is the much larger value of our exports than the value of our imports. In 1938 our sales to Europe were $1,297 million but our purchases were only $564 million.

The United Kingdom

While this disparity has characterized our trade with both continental Europe and the United Kingdom, it has been most pronounced in the case of the United Kingdom. Our exports to the United Kingdom in 1938 had a value of $521 million while our imports amounted to only $118 million.[1]

In view of this prewar trend plus the special difficulties resulting from the war, British preoccupation with their balance of payments in relation to the United States can readily be understood.[2] A net bilateral balance between the two countries would be neither practicable nor normal. Nevertheless, so large a disparity does present a rather difficult problem in multilateral balance.

This needs to be kept in mind to understand the extreme position of one group in the United Kingdom, that argues that a return to foreign trade without strict state control will prove impossible. This group places its confidence in the bargaining power of the United Kingdom as a great consuming market in negotiating bilateral agreements. The formation of a sterling bloc is also envisaged.

The relative shift of our trade away from Europe as a market and as a source of supply reflects the changed productive character of our country. We were as a nation a

[1] "Summary of Foreign Trade of the United States, Calendar Year 1940," pp. 9, 12.
[2] See pp. 90–97 for a discussion of our protective tariff and the pound-dollar ratio in connection with the problem of balance of payments.

manufactures importer, a raw-materials exporter. We have reversed our role and become dominantly a manufactures exporter, a raw-materials importer. No doubt, our protective tariff was a factor in the change, but the trend, on a larger or smaller scale, was practically inevitable.

Latin America

The percentage of our imports coming from Latin America did not vary materially from 1900 to 1940, remaining somewhat above 20 per cent. The percentage of our exports to Latin America, however, about 10 per cent at the beginning of the century, was roughly 19 per cent by 1937. In dollar value, our exports to Latin America in this period increased more than four times.

Thus the balance of trade with Latin America underwent a significant change. Previously, we bought much more from Latin American countries than we sold them. By the outbreak of the present war, our exports to and our imports from Latin America were approaching a balance. During the war, the pendulum has swung back, and we are again importing much more from that area than we are exporting to it. This situation is caused by temporary wartime factors, however, and affords no ground for forecasts.

The industrialization of Latin America, apparently under way on a large scale and at an accelerated pace, will mean increased demand for capital equipment as well as for durable consumers' goods, such as automobiles and electrical appliances. Our future trade with Latin America will, however, be affected by political factors. It is apparent that the industrialization of Latin America is accompanied by a growth of economic nationalism, which foreshadows an effort to keep industrial management and control in the hands of their own nationals. Our participation is likely to be confined to selling (and installing) capital equipment, to furnishing technical aid during the early stages, and, perhaps, to lending funds. Outright American ownership and operation of the newly established industries seems improbable on any considerable scale.

Canada

Our trade with Canada becomes increasingly important. Canada's percentage of our exports rose from 13.7 per cent in 1911–1915 to 15.1 per cent in 1938. In our imports the increase is even more pronounced, since we took 8 per cent from Canada in 1911–1915 and 13.3 per cent in 1938. During this period the value of our exports to Canada has exceeded substantially the value of our imports from Canada. In the recent war years this disparity has been corrected, but this position may not be retained after the war, when the balance will probably be "in our favor" again.

Soviet Russia

Undoubtedly, Soviet Russia will wish to import capital equipment in large amounts in order to erase the ravages of the war and to continue the industrialization of the country. It is important, however, to examine against the background of pertinent statistics the optimistic expectations expressed by some concerning postwar trade with Russia.

In 1937 total Soviet imports from all countries amounted to $268 millions,[1] exports amounted to $346 million. In the same year the United States imported goods and services valued at over $3 billion and exported a total of $3.3 billion. In other words, the sum of our imports from all countries was more than eleven times as great as Soviet imports from all countries while our exports were almost ten times as large.

In 1937, Soviet imports from the United States amounted to roughly $43 million. Exports from Russia to the United

[1] United States Department of Commerce, Bureau of Foreign and Domestic Commerce, *Foreign Commerce Yearbook*, 1938, U.S. Government Printing Office, Washington, D.C., 1939, p. 168. Imports had been somewhat more than half a billion dollars in 1930 and 1931, when capital equipment for the first Five Year Plan was purchased. They fell to about $200 million in 1934.

States during the same year amounted to about $31 million.[1] In other words, our exports to Russia in 1937 were about 1.5 per cent of our total exports, and our imports from Russia were less than 1 per cent of our total imports.

This extremely low level of trade between the United States and Soviet Russia, and, indeed, between Soviet Russia and the rest of the world, was primarily due to the policy of economic self-sufficiency followed by the Soviet government. The existence of a huge continental free-trade area under the Soviet flag renders such a policy practicable. The ratio of foreign trade to national income has been below even that of the United States.

Relations of Soviet Russia with her capitalistic Allies are far more friendly today than they were before the war. The ever-imminent attack by Germany or Japan will not face her for some time, if ever again. Soviet economic policy may conceivably be less autarchical after the war than it was before and, consequently, the level of possible American exports to Russia might approach that under lend-lease rather than that of prewar commercial trade. But it does not seem likely that Soviet Russia will abandon her traditional economic policy, one that has served her well, for a totally different one. There is no prospect that the foreign-trade monopoly will be abolished, since this is a fundamental part of the economic system. Of course, such a trade monopoly can readily make effective a changed governmental economic policy and enlarged imports and exports if an increased foreign trade were considered in the national interest.

There is every reason to believe that exports to Russia will be very large for a period of two or three years while reconstruction is being carried on and while credit is available. It

[1] United States Department of Commerce, Bureau of Foreign and Domestic Commerce, Division of Foreign Trade Statistics, *The Foreign Commerce and Navigation of the United States, Calendar Year* 1939, U.S. Government Printing Office, Washington, D.C., 1940, Table VI, p. XV.

is reported that the Soviet government has requested a post-war credit of $6 billion from the United States government. The Soviet government is entitled to a high credit rating, based upon the record of payments of foreign commercial obligations over a long period of years. But expansion of our trade with Russia to a level comparable to our trade with France, for example, would present problems for which solutions are not yet apparent.

One of the greatest hindrances to such a development would be finding export commodities from which Soviet Russia could obtain the foreign exchange to pay for a large volume of imports from the United States or to repay credits advanced. Exports of manganese, lumber, pulp wood, asbestos, furs, coal, sausage casings, fish and caviar, matches, and other products have been utterly inadequate to finance large imports. Though some dollar exchange could be earned through the sale of timber, grain, petroleum products, and foodstuffs on the European market, the net amounts of exchange remaining, after paying for imports from Europe, would not cover large purchases from the United States.

Furthermore, Russia has shown a noticeable tendency to increase domestic consumption of staple products formerly exported. Thus the enlarged petroleum production during the late 1930's was not enough to take care of the greatly expanded domestic consumption, and petroleum exports were curtailed. Essentially the same thing was true of wheat.

Reduction of the current large expenditures for national defense may release resources to produce goods for export, which would serve to increase considerably the means of payment for imports. Finally, Russian gold can be used to pay for imports. Exact figures on Russian gold production are not available, but over $100 million annually might be readily expected from this source. All this gold would, however, by no means be available for purchases in the United States.

In the long perspective, it seems likely that our trade with

Soviet Russia will be considerably larger than in prewar years. Should the United States government grant large credits to Russia, our exports during the immediate postwar years might be very large indeed. But how these credits could be repaid in goods when they come due and what would replace the credits after they were exhausted is not yet clear.

SUMMARY

The immediate prospect after the end of the war with Germany is for a strong export demand for our products. Adequate gold holdings and dollar exchange exist in almost all neutral countries, in Latin America, and even among some of the belligerents. The most pressing problems arise from the weak British balance-of-payments position, and out of the blocked sterling balances, such as the debt of £1 billion to India. The Axis countries will, of course, be without any substantial means of payment. The general situation should be greatly improved if the International Monetary Fund and the International Bank for Reconstruction and Development can begin operations shortly after Germany's defeat.

There has been a continuing shift in the commodity structure of our import-export trade. We are becoming more and more an exporter of manufactured goods and an importer of raw materials. To the extent that this has been caused by our protective tariff, a change toward freer international trade might check the trend but is not likely to reverse it.

There has been a relative shift away from trade with Europe, although Europe remains our best customer. Our trade with Latin America, with Oceania, and with Southeastern Asia has been expanding. Whether this geographical trend away from trade with Europe will continue is not certain. Trade with Latin America may grow with the industrialization of its countries. Trade with Oceania and Southeastern Asia may be limited by developments in our production of synthetic rubber and fibers. Trade with

Russia is likely to increase but, without very large export credits, may not reach levels that would make it a major factor in our total exports.

It has been estimated that, with a gross national product of $175 billion (attainable at full production within two or three years after the end of the war), our imports—as well as our exports—might reach a total of $7 billion.[1] This would mean doubling the dollar value of exports from their 1937 level and more than a doubling of imports. Foreign trade at that level also implies a national income for the United States approximately twice in dollar value that of 1937.[2] This estimate of foreign trade is based simply upon past relationships between gross national product and our foreign trade. It is patently not feasible to foretell how much more trade would follow initiation of a program for expanding foreign trade and synchronized national programs of full employment. Both imports and exports would be greatly stimulated. It would be well to recognize that even the volume of imports and exports estimated may not be attainable without a comprehensive program of international economic cooperation. The combination of substantially full employment in all countries and expanded international trade would make it possible to attain and maintain the highest possible levels of national income. The opportunity now exists; it may not offer again.

[1] See *Foreign Trade after the War.*

[2] On account of differences in price levels between 1937 and the postwar years the increase in quantities would represent substantially less than doubling of either national income or foreign trade.

A NOTE ON
THE COMMITTEE FOR ECONOMIC DEVELOPMENT
AND ITS RESEARCH PROGRAM

The Committee for Economic Development was organized in August, 1942, by a group of business leaders who were convinced that the attainment and maintenance of high employment after the war dare not be left to chance. To seize the opportunities for unprecedented peacetime prosperity in the postwar era and to avoid the real perils of mass unemployment or mass government employment, they believed that individual employers, while in no degree relaxing their efforts toward military victory, must begin to plan promptly, realistically, and boldly for rapid reconversion and vigorous expansion after the war.

There is widespread agreement among economists that American prosperity after the war calls for the sustained employment of 7 to 10 million more workers than in 1940, our banner peacetime year hitherto. The only sound road to such increased employment is the enlargement of production and sales of goods and services to a level some 30 to 45 per cent higher than that of 1940. This means that businessmen must make their plans for postwar business on a greatly expanded basis as compared to any known peacetime year.

To assist them to make their maximum contribution toward this goal, the Committee for Economic Development—through its Field Development Division—has organized locally (as of June, 1945) in more than 2,800 counties and communities in all states of the union. More than 50,000 businessmen are working as members of these committees to persuade and aid as many as possible of the nation's 2 million private employers to begin the planning of their postwar production and employment.

No pattern or over-all program is imposed on these local committees. Each is autonomous, since each understands the peculiar problems of its community better than can any outsider. Yet the problems they meet and the tools they need are in basic respects the same.

Therefore, tested procedures for making both postwar production and employment plans are supplied to them by the national C.E.D. office. In addition, the country's outstanding specialists in industrial management, in product design, in advertising and selling, and in training of sales personnel have placed their skills freely at the service of all cooperating businessmen, through handbooks, films, training courses, business clinics, and forums for the local committees.

To plan for the future, the businessman needs particularly some measure for estimating postwar demand for his individual product. Another important service of C.E.D. is its postwar market analysis, which is being conducted with the cooperation of many trade associations and leading industrial firms and will cover more than 500 finished-goods products.

Even with the best of tools the businessman knows he cannot be wholly successful in carrying out plans for postwar expansion unless national policies prevail that make business expansion possible. To define what these national policies of government, business, and labor should be to encourage higher production and more jobs is the special task of the C.E.D. Research Division. This is the purpose of the research reports, of which this volume is the fifth.

To the long-range economic questions involved in this undertaking have been added the particular economic problems arising out of the war. Both areas are being studied. It is hoped that the reports, as a group, will provide the information that many have been seeking concerning problems intimately related to the life of each of us, as well as to the future of our society.

The authors of these reports have already won distinction in their own fields. Perhaps more important is the fact that their previous work has demonstrated not only the competence but the vigor of thought which these complex problems demand. Knowing, however, that the problems that would be scrutinized—demobilization of the war economy, taxation, monetary policy, international trade, agriculture, and the like—are not separate ones, but are integrated and must be studied in relationship one to the other, the C.E.D. sought to make possible an exchange of information and views by the experts and, equally important, between the scholars and businessmen.

What may be a unique scheme of conferences was established, the objective being to blend the practical experience and judgment of the business world with the scholars' knowledge of the action of economic forces. A Research Committee consisting of representative successful businessmen was set up; to this group was added a Research Advisory Board whose members are recognized as among our leading social scientists; and, finally, the persons who would be responsible for the individual reports were named, to comprise the Research Staff.

The subject matter of each report is discussed by the members of these three groups, meeting together. "Discussed" is an inadequate term. "Earnestly argued, and for long hours" does more justice to the work. The author of the report therefore has the benefit of criticism and suggestion by many other competent minds. He is able to follow closely the development of the reports on other economic matters that affect his own study.

No effort is made to arrive at absolute agreement. There is no single answer to the problems that are being studied. What is gained is agreement as to the determinative factors in each problem, and the possible results to be achieved by differing methods of handling the problem. The author of the report has full responsibility, and complete freedom, for proposing whatever action or solution seems advisable to him. There is only one rule—the approach must be from the standpoint of the general welfare and not from that of any special economic or political group; the objective must be high production and high employment in a democratic society.

Since the author is free to present his own conclusions and does not speak for the Research Committee or for the Research Advisory Board, the Research Committee will issue, for each study, where desirable, a separate C.E.D. *policy statement.* This may endorse all of the recommendations arrived at by the author, or it may disagree with some.

The research studies already under way divide roughly into two parts:

A. *The transition from war to peace:* the problems involved in the early *attainment* of high levels of employment and production when the war is over;

B. *The longer term fundamental problems* involved in the *maintenance* of high levels of productive employment after the transition period has passed.

The subjects to be covered by the individual monographs in the two series are:

A. *The Transition from War to Peace:*

1. *The Liquidation of War Production,* by A. D. H. Kaplan, The Brookings Institution (already published). The problems involved in the cancellation of war contracts and the disposal of government-owned surplus supplies, plants, and capital equipment are weighed quantitatively as well as qualitatively. How much war plant has the government financed, and what part of it could be put into civilian production? What criteria should prevail in selecting the producers to be released first from war manufactures, as the war-production program is curtailed? How and when should surplus goods be sold? Rapid resumption of peace-

time production, with conditions favorable to high levels of employment, is the gauge by which the recommendations are measured.

2. *Demobilization of Wartime Economic Controls*, by John Maurice Clark, Professor of Economics, Columbia University (already published). When and how should the wartime controls be removed? The interdependency of the wartime controls of production, manpower, prices, wages, rationing, credit policies, and others is made clear. How relaxation of each control may affect the peacetime economy —in terms of demand and supply, and therefore in terms of job and production levels—is weighed. The conditions that can be expected to prevail at different stages of the transition from a wartime to a peacetime economy are outlined, with emphasis on the variables with which we must be prepared to deal. Professor Clark does not overlook the significance of attitudes and objectives.

3. *Manpower Demobilization and Reemployment*, by Robert R. Nathan, Consulting Economist, and Emmett H. Welch, Chief, Economic Statistics Unit, Bureau of the Census. The relationship of demobilization policy to reemployment. Recommendations are made for a program that would avoid long-period joblessness among returning servicemen as well as war workers.

4. *Providing for Unemployed Workers in the Transition*, by Richard A. Lester, Associate Professor of Economics, Duke University (already published). An estimate of the size and the duration of transition unemployment. The efficacy of public works employment, relief employment, the adequacy of unemployment compensation, wartime savings, dismissal pay, and the like are appraised. A program is developed to provide for the maintenance of workers who will be out of jobs in the transition from war to peace.

5. *Financing Industry during the Transition from War to Peace*, by Charles C. Abbott, Associate Professor of Business Economics, Harvard University. The sources upon which business has relied for its capital are examined, along with the current financial condition of large and small corporations. These two are weighed against the likely needs of financing by industry for reconversion and expansion in the transition years following the war.

6. *Monetary and Banking Policies in the Postwar Transition Period*, by John K. Langum, Vice-president, Federal Reserve Bank of Chicago. What monetary and banking policies can do to encourage production and employment. Federal fiscal policy is analyzed in its relationship to the financial requirements of business in reconversion and expansion. The significance of monetary policies prior to the war and the money and banking conditions that will stem from war financing are reviewed. The relationship of business spending to other money flows and the resultant production pattern are discussed.

B. *The Longer term Fundamental Problems:*

1. *Production, Jobs and Taxes*, by Harold M. Groves, Professor of Economics, University of Wisconsin (already published). A study of the federal tax structure as it affects the creation of jobs. This is to be followed by a comprehensive report now in preparation on the development of a constructive tax policy. The larger report will inquire into the problems of state and local, as well as federal, taxation.

2. *Agriculture in an Unstable Economy*, by Theodore W. Schultz, Professor of Agricultural Economics, The University of Chicago. An investigation going to the roots of the "farm problem." The significance

of excess labor resources on farms, the failure of price mechanisms to induce shifts of resources out of agriculture, the differences between the farm and industrial sectors in responding to reduced demand. The importance to farmers of continued prosperity in business. A solution to the farm problem without resort to price floors or restrictions on output.

3. *International Trade and Domestic Employment*, by Calvin B. Hoover, Dean of the Graduate School of Arts and Sciences, Duke University (the present volume). An examination of the kind of foreign-trade policies and mechanisms we can adopt that will increase our gains from international trade and also contribute to world peace. A statement of the requirements in terms of the economies of other countries as well as our own.

4. *Business Arrangements in Foreign Trade*, by Edward S. Mason, Professor of Economics, Harvard University. A study of cartels and other forms of international business organizations.

5. *Minimizing Business Fluctuations and Unemployment*, a major series of studies which will be undertaken during the coming year, by John Maurice Clark, K. E. Boulding, M. de Chazeau, Albert G. Hart, Gardiner C. Means, Howard B. Myers, Theodore O. Yntema, and others to be appointed.

6. *The Special Problems of Small Business*, by A. D. H. Kaplan, The Brookings Institution, assisted by J. K. Wexman. An inquiry into the competitive position and the needs of small business.

7. *Providing Adequate Incentives for Enterprise*, by C. E. Griffin, Professor of Business Economics, University of Michigan.

8. *The "Billion Dollar Questions."* By Theodore O. Yntema, Gardiner C. Means, and Howard B. Myers. An economic primer posing the basic economic problems to be faced in a free-enterprise system.

C. *Supplementary Papers:*

1. *The Economics of a Free Society,* by William Benton, Chairman of the Board, Encyclopaedia Britannica, Inc. (Published in October, 1944, issue of *Fortune Magazine.*)
2. *Personnel Problems of the Postwar Transition Period,* by Charles A. Myers, Assistant Professor of Industrial Relations, Massachusetts Institute of Technology (already published). An examination of the problems that will confront employers in connection with the rehiring of servicemen and war workers, and issues that will arise in the shift of the work force from wartime to peacetime production.
3. *Federal Tax Reform,* by Henry C. Simons, Associate Professor of Economics, The University of Chicago. The development of a basic philosophy of taxation to simplify the federal tax structure and distribute the tax burden among individuals in relation to their incomes.
4. *Incidence of Taxation,* by William Vickrey, formerly Tax Research Division, Treasury Department.
5. *World Politics, Employment and Free Private Enterprise,* by Harold Lasswell, Director of War Communications Research, Library of Congress.
6. *Changes in Substantive Law, Legal Processes and Government Organization to Maintain Conditions Favorable to Competition,* by Corwin Edwards, Professor of Economics, Northwestern University.

These are the subjects so far authorized by the Research Committee of C.E.D. Others may be undertaken at a later date. These subject titles will not necessarily be the same as the book titles when finally published.

EXCERPTS FROM BY-LAWS OF THE COMMITTEE
FOR ECONOMIC DEVELOPMENT CONCERNING
THE RESEARCH PROGRAM

Section 3. Research Committee.

It shall be the responsibility of the Research Committee to initiate studies into the principles of business policy and of public policy which will foster the full contribution by industry and commerce in the post-war period to the attainment of high and secure standards of living for people in all walks of life through maximum employment and high productivity in the domestic economy. All research is to be thoroughly objective in character, and the approach in each instance is to be from the standpoint of the general welfare and not from that of any special political or economic group.

Publication

The determination of whether or not a study shall be published shall rest solely with the Research Director and the Research Advisory Board. . . . A copy of any manuscript reported for publication shall be submitted to each member of the Research Advisory Board, of the Research Committee, of the Board of Trustees, and to the Chairman and Vice-chairmen of the Field Development Committee. For each subject to be so submitted the Research Director, after consulting with the Chairman of the Research Advisory Board, shall appoint a Reading Committee of three members of the Board. Thereupon, as a special assignment each member of the Reading Committee shall read the manuscript and within fifteen days from its assignment to him shall signify his approval or disapproval for publication. If two out of the three Reading Committee members signify their approval, the manuscript shall be published at the expense of the Corporation. . . . In no case shall publication necessarily constitute endorsement by the Committee for Economic Development, the Board of Trustees, the Research Committee or by the Research Advisory Board of the manuscript's conclusions. Upon approval for publication, the Research Director shall notify all members of the Research Advisory Board and no manuscript may be published until fifteen days following such notification. The interval is allowed for the receipt of any memorandum of comment, reservation or dissent that any member of the Research Advisory Board may wish to express. Should a member of the Research Advisory Board so request, his memorandum of comment, reservation or dissent, which must be signed, shall be published with the manuscript. Any signed comment, reservation or dissent which the Research Director may wish to express or have expressed by others shall at his request be published with the manuscript. . . . In the event the manuscript is not approved for publication at the Corporation's expense as above provided, the individual or group making the research shall nevertheless have the right to publish the manuscript.

Supplementary Papers

The Research Director may recommend to the Editorial Board for publication as a Supplementary Paper any manuscript (other than a regular research report) . . . which in his opinion should be made publicly available because it constitutes an important contribution to the understanding of a problem on which research has been initiated by the Research Committee.

An Editorial Board for Supplementary Papers shall be established consisting of five members: The Research Director, two members from the Research Committee, and two members from the Research Advisory Board. The members from the Research Committee and the members from the Research Advisory Board shall be appointed by the respective chairmen of those bodies. The Research Director shall be the chairman of the Editorial Board and shall act as Editor of the Supplementary Papers. . . . If a majority of the members of the Editorial Board vote for publication, the manuscript shall be published as one of a series of Supplementary Papers, separate and distinct from the regular research reports. . . . Publication does not constitute endorsement of the author's statements by the Committee for Economic Development, by the Board of Trustees, by the Research Committee, or by the Research Advisory Board.

RESEARCH COMMITTEE

RESEARCH ADVISORY BOARD

INDEX

Index

Index